Cycling the Camino de Santiago

Ken Scott

First Edition 2019 Fortis Publishing Services

Copyright © Fortis Publishing under exclusive licence from Ken Scott.

The rights of Ken Scott have been asserted in accordance with the Copyright, Designs and Patents Act 1998.
No part of this book may be reprinted or reproduced or utilised in any form or by any electronic, mechanical, or other means, now known or hereafter invented, including photocopying and recording, or in any information storage or retrieval system, without permission in writing from the publishers.

ISBN-13: 9781702299688

Fortis Publishing
Kemp House
160 City Road
London
EC1V 2NX

To Tommy & Irene
Always with me wherever my journey takes me.

Ken Scott has written or collaborated on nearly thirty books. He is a published author, ghost-writer and writing coach and a contributor to The Huffington Post.

Author of:

Jack of Hearts
A Million Would Be Nice
The Sun Will Still Shine Tomorrow
Families At War

Ghost-writer & Collaborator

Revenge is Sweeter than Flowing Honey - Crissy Rock
Race Against Me -Dwain Chambers
Who The Hell is Alice? Alice Barry
This Heart Within Me Burns - Crissy Rock
Do The Birds Still Sing In Hell? - Horace Greasley
The Blue Door - Lise Kristensen
Sherlock's Squadron - Steve Holmes
Fitted Up But Fighting Back - Kevin Lane
Call Me Mistress - Jessica Black
The Genesis Chamber - Beighton Devlin
In Violet Sleep - Peter Ridsdale
The Gate That Cried Blood - Geoff Nordass
The Devil Couldn't Break Me - Laura Aslan
The Survivor - Felipe Albero Gomez
Whatever Happened to Jan Rose Kasmir? - Jan Rose Kasmir

Undercover in a Jihad Training Camp - Jibril Jacobs
The Cooking Pot - Reinette Visser - Emily Douglas - Ken Scott
And then the Penny Dropped - BP Kennedy
Not all Robbers Wear a Mask - Jessica E Summers

Ken Scott
www.kenscottbooks.com

Fortis Publishing
www.fortispublishing.co.uk

Introduction

One of the reasons for writing this book was that I struggled to find anything suitable to read before our 1000 km Camino Cycle Challenge.

The walkers and hikers are spoiled for choice with plenty of books covering all the different routes and pilgrims have penned millions of words over the years. There are tales of the journey, detailed routes, historical facts and some outstanding after-dinner reading while nursing those blisters with a cold beer. And their bible, A Pilgrims Guide by John Brierley, seems to be carried by most pilgrims along The Way. There are thousands of walking books about the Camino for sale on Amazon, but for we cyclists, there´s very little indeed. More so, I didn't want to produce a guide because, with the help of our good friend Google Maps and a decent GPS signal, anyone can get from point A to point B nowadays.

There were a few books penned by the two-wheeled enthusiasts over the years and I and bought some of them, only to find them disappointing due to lack of content. Only Mike Wells´ book is substantial enough, I think.

What exactly was I looking for? Well, first of all, I looked to see if any other cyclists had chosen the route from Bordeaux to Santiago de Compostela. I wanted to read how they fared. No doubt there have been thousands of two-wheelers over the years, but it appears nobody has taken the time to sit down and write about their cycling experiences from Bordeaux or even from Paris or Tours. There is nothing about the route I'd chosen and nothing specific about a 1000 km challenge which was strange because France has always been the traditional starting point for the Camino.

I wanted to hear of my fellow cyclists´ experiences with GPS, Map my Ride or Strava and to hear if anyone had plotted their route the old-fashioned way, with a paper map. I wanted to know where to stay, where to eat and what pitfalls to look out for combined with a decent word count and a story of the journey. In other words, I wanted to get to know the people who I would be reading about, much in the same way a decent fiction book takes you into the mindset of the protagonist. What were they thinking, where were they heading, what drove them on and made them continue on their adventure right to the very end? I desperately wanted more than just a pamphlet or a guide.

I wanted the highs and lows, stories about days that didn't go so well and, of course, the uplifting tales of spiritual awakenings, of nature, of the history of the Camino and of the camaraderie with their fellow man.

So I took along no more than my mobile phone with a voice recorder app to record everything along The Way, and wrote it up when I returned home. I also took a copy of ´My Camino Journal´ by Reinette Visser. It´s a well-structured journal and I found it useful in the evenings as I wrote up my notes and made references to places and people we met along the way.

The Camino de Santiago has everything; it truly is the experience of a lifetime and I am happy to say the highs far outnumbered the lows. I decided I would write about the characters we met, the acts of kindness and of the occasional serious, and not so serious, mishap – of which we had plenty.

Cycling the Camino throws up the odd drama, from punctures and accidents to getting thrown onto a dirt track that leads nowhere, and it tests your patience and brings out the best and the worst in you.

I wrote this book because I believe there isn't another book specifically aimed at cyclists who want to put in serious mileage on the Camino de Santiago.

This book will tell you about pre-Camino training and preparation and about what kit you should and shouldn't pack. It's about travelling as light as possible because dragging 25 kg of bike and kit up a 1500 m climb isn´t much fun and saps your energy like you wouldn't believe. Oh, how I envied the cyclists who passed us on feather-light racing bikes, carrying no more kit than a couple of bottles of water and a light daypack or saddlebag.

This book is not an expert's view on how to complete a 1000 km cycle challenge. Far from it - it was our first attempt at this sort of adventure and only by doing it and writing everything down do we learn from our mistakes. And boy did we make some mistakes. One of our gang quipped that I should name this book 'How not to Cycle the Camino,' and there's a wee bit of truth in that. At times it was like the blind leading the blind and yet, that added to our adventure. Hopefully, before you set off on wherever your journey takes you, you will read and learn.

This book is aimed at the person who loves cycling but doesn't want to kill themselves with exhaustion on a daily basis. That's not to say we didn't have some killer days and you will read about those days in due course.

Our biggest mistake was that we probably cycled too many kilometres each day. Our group was 50 years plus, the oldest being 57 and there was only one 'club' man in our group. The rest of us, although reasonably fit, are only casual cyclists who get out just once or twice a week. We enjoy our cycling, but we don't bust a gut to hit targets or cycle until our bodies cry for mercy.

The good news is that it's achievable and if we can do it, anyone can.

On reflection, I would probably have cut a couple of hundred kilometres from our route and taken at least one more rest day. Cutting out a few hundred kilometres and starting from Saint-Jean-Pied-de-Port would have been a more sensible option, but be warned, it makes for a lot of climbing early on.
Alternatively, turning our two-week trip into a three-week trip would have been far more enjoyable.

I have described five possible routes in this book. I detail the options and the climbs and there are a few tips on how to cut out a lot of ascent even though it may add a few kilometres to your cycling day. You may very well love hills, and I do, but climbing day after day with your head down is not the ideal way to enjoy the spectacular scenery.

In Part Two, I will give you lots of practical tips and advice like how to get your bike home again in one piece, hassle-free.

I will introduce you to our gang in Part One. I go into their characters and their personalities and of how difficult it was for each of them individually. And above all, I write about how much fun we had and how we laughed from start to finish, no matter what the gods threw at us. That, in my opinion, is the only way through the 'dark days.'

I will finish this introduction with some good advice.

Everybody has their own personal Camino challenge. It's not about how many kilometres you walk or cycle or how many hills you can get over. We met a Belgian man, Jan Vandersypen, who was cycling 2,200 km from his hometown in Belgium. He said everyone has their own Camino, whether they walk 50 km or cycle 2,000 km. It's not about the route or the time. Don't be frightened to deviate your route if it saves a little time or cuts out a few hundred metres elevation or if it takes you to a splendid little hotel. Don't become obsessed with following trails or heading for cities just because the ancient Romans went there a few hundred years ago. The Camino is a personal thing; it's where YOU want to go.

This pilgrimage is now so popular that little routes are branching off every year and that's great because it cuts down on the people traffic. It's as if your journey becomes your very own personal track to Santiago. You will crisscross the Camino wherever you go, meet up with your fellow travellers at the *albergues* or campsites *en route* and you will find that everyone has their own agenda. That's the beauty of The Way; it's yours to tailor as you wish.

Our Journey

The first part of the book is the fun part about our adventure into the great unknown. Make no mistake, it was tough. This was a serious endeavour that pushed us to the limit and we are all fairly fit. You will read about the banter, the alcohol intake, the disagreements and the disaster days. There's also some good advice about diet and resting and the precautions you need to take each day if you want to make it to Santiago without having to take an ambulance.

Now, without further ado let me introduce you to our protagonists.

Meet the Gang

There were originally about 12 members of our Camino group, but one by one, during the training period they fell by the wayside, leaving only four of us.

Ken Scott

I'm an author and a ghost-writer and started cycling around five years ago. I live on the beautiful Costa Blanca in Spain, and after deciding that my amateur football career was over, I bought a 'supermarket' bike, the kind you see on offer in Asda at Christmas for a 100 quid, because I wanted to see a little more of the mountains and countryside where I live. Within a few weeks the cycling bug bit me and I haven´t stopped cycling since.

The Camino Challenge was my idea. Why not, I said to myself; a thousand kilometres is a nice round figure and surely it can't be that hard.

I'd been talking to my best mate Dave, in England, who'd had a cancer scare and decided he wanted a challenge - something to test him before he got much older. At first, we flirted with a trip to Everest Base Camp, but the more we read about it, the more we realised that we needed something a bit more sensible. It is expensive and difficult to get to and the research we did told us that the mountain is so busy, it´s like the tube station at Piccadilly Circus.

We began looking at other options and challenges and because I remembered that Dave had started cycling too, I suggested the Camino de Santiago and we began planning.

Dave would probably tell you that I'm

headstrong, opinionated and bossy and that I like my own way. It's probably true, I'm not going to argue with him.

At the time of the Camino Challenge, I was 56 years old, I weighed 86kg - a little overweight - and I cycled two or three times a week. My rides averaged about 50 km and were always in the mountains nearby. As my good buddy John Macaulay keeps telling me, hills are my friends.

It's true; I love the hills. I love pushing myself up hills and mountains and I get an enormous sense of achievement once I reach the top, especially if there´s a bar serving ice-cold beer.

Weakness – beer
Pet hate - negative people who waste time and energy moaning
Hobbies apart from cycling - Newcastle United
Nicknames - Scotty, Dickens, the Beer Monster.

Gary Jackson

Gary is the most laid-back bloke I have ever met on planet earth. He is an HGV driver in Newcastle, where he´s lived all his life. I met Gary at Chillingham Road Primary School when I was six years old and we´ve been friends ever since. Gary is the salt of the earth. He will do anything for you and if you are in his immediate family or classed as one of his close friends, he will never let you down. Gary is the only club cyclist in the group, cycling once or twice a week in a peloton and he also cycles to work and back every day. Gary is around 5' 6'' and rotund but as strong as an ox and will tell you that if you put him on a bike, he may not be very fast, but he will cycle all day without stopping. He proved that several times during the Challenge.

Weakness – spending money
Pet hate – spending money
Hobbies apart from cycling – his family, but especially his grandchildren
Nicknames- Jacko, the Whatever Man

Caroline Rankin

Caroline was the only chica in our group and also the youngest. I have known Caroline for several years; I think our paths crossed while walking our dogs along the same routes. She also lives here on the Costa Blanca.

I had been out cycling close to where we live one day and, as usual, I stopped at the local bar for a beer after my ride. Caroline was in there and the conversation went something like this:

"Hi, Ken."

"Caroline, how are you?"

"Great, what you been up to?"

"Just been cycling."

"A bit hot," she said.

"Nah," I said, "I'm used to it."

"Where have you been?"

"Guadalest."

"No way, that's all uphill, it's hard enough driving up there in the car."

"Hills are my friends."

So we discussed the ride and eventually I got around to telling her that my mates and I were thinking about cycling the Camino de Santiago.

"I would love to do that," she said.

"Then join us," I replied.

"I'm in the gang."

"It's a thousand kilometres," I said.

She turned white and whispered, "how many?"

"Do you cycle?" I asked.
She shook her head.
"Do you have a bike?"
She shook her head again.
"When did you last sit on a bicycle?"
"When I was fourteen."
We sat for an hour. I tried to talk her out of it and nearly managed it when I said we would be camping most of the time. She told me she hated camping with a passion and couldn't think of anything worse. She doesn´t go anywhere without a hairdryer and being the glam chick that she is, I emphasised to her how light we would have to travel.
"Ten kilos max," I said.
"How much is that?"
"Smaller than the wheelie case you take on a Ryanair flight."
"For two weeks?"
"Yes, and waterproofs, spare tubes, a toolkit, sleeping bag and a tent make up about seven of those ten kilos."
"No way, so I only have three kilos for myself?"
I nodded.
"No hairdryer then."
"No."
I told her to think about it. Everything conspired against her; she didn't cycle, she had no bike and camping was the last thing in the world she wanted to do.
We said goodbye. That's the last I'm going to hear from her I thought to myself.

Twenty-four hours later, she called me. "I need to buy a bike," she said, "I'm in the gang."

Caroline is lovely. She´s tall, elegant and pretty and she´s the life and soul of any party, but she´s prone to hissy fits at the end of a hard-cycling day and if things don´t go her way. Do not stand in her way at this point and do not think that any words will console her or calm her down. They won't. Just point her in the direction of a glass of wine and come back an hour later when she has refuelled on Rioja.

Weakness - wine
Pet hate - cycling up hills
Hobbies apart from cycling - hiking and walking the dogs
Nicknames – Blondie, Mine's a Wine

Dave Graham

I have also known Dave since school, so it's fair to say we go back a long way. I shared a flat with him and as young men in our twenties, we rode around on motorbikes and shared many other hobbies such as football, hiking and a love of the Newcastle pub life. As a Geordie, he is also a big Newcastle United fan.

Dave is 57 years of age, retired, and lives on the north-east coast with his partner Jill and he likes things to be perfect. I think the term OCD was invented for the exact way to describe him. As the thesaurus explains, "A tendency towards orderliness, perfectionism and attention to detail."

I laughed when we rolled up at one apartment we had booked in the south of France where we were all staying on one floor. There was a small lounge with an occasional table in a corner of the room. Almost as soon as we walked through the door, Dave laid claim to the table and placed all his personal possessions neatly on top.

"I'll claim this corner of the room," he said, so obsessed was he to line his stuff up just as he wanted it, not realising that it was the only bloody table in the place.

That's Dave, things have to be right, schedules kept to and if we agree to set off at eight o'clock the next morning, woe betide anyone who isn't ready.

Dave is also one determined bugger, just the kind

of person you need to call upon on a challenge like this. He will not give up. Even though there were a couple of days where he was running on fumes and he wanted to call it a day, it was never going to happen. You will read all about his determination (and stubbornness) in subsequent chapters and there were some great ding dongs between Caroline and him. Come to think about it; I had some great ding dongs with Caroline and one or two with Dave. Could it be me who has the problem?

Dave loves his tennis and is a very good club player and like me, only started cycling in recent years. He stepped up his mileage significantly in recent months in order to get fit for this challenge. We spent a week together at my place, at a training camp six weeks prior to the challenge. He agrees that the Costa Blanca is the greatest place in the world for cyclists.

Dave was diagnosed with bladder cancer in 2018 and had an operation to remove a tumour. He does not require any further treatment, so fingers crossed that it was just that, a scare.

Weaknesses - He talks for England. Very indecisive; make sure you have a spare half hour when you walk into a bar because that's how long it will take him to choose a drink.

Pet hates - Litter. People who are arc welded to their mobile phones. Mike Ashley.

Hobbies apart from cycling - Newcastle United, Tennis, Bird watching.

Nicknames - Pete Perfect, Wavey Davey.

Bordeaux or Bust

Before we get to Bordeaux it's worth taking a couple of paragraphs to look at the bikes, the kit you will need and more importantly, how to get them there if you have decided against hiring locally.

Bike Hire

We decided against hiring bikes because of the cost and the fact that we struggled to find a hire company where we could pick up a bike from anywhere near Bordeaux. We thought we had found a company that, for a small charge, would transport the bikes from their depot in Toulouse to Bordeaux and collect them again in Santiago. The cost of hiring bikes for two weeks was 350€. What?! That's 25€ a day; I can hire a decent race bike from my local shop for 15€. It got worse; they wanted another 50€ to transport each bike to Bordeaux.

I was gobsmacked at the cost as I had expected it to be half that, so it was time to look at flying our own bikes to Bordeaux. It's fair to say that dismantling and boxing up a bike is a bit of a hassle, but for 65€, flying Ryanair, you get a whopping 30kg weight allowance in your box, which allows for the bike and tools with a sleeping bag and tent. Don't forget you have to dump your box at the other end so don't spend a small fortune on the coolest, latest carry case even if it only weighs three or four kilos. It's bulky and you don't want that additional weight on your bike. The best advice I can give is to go to your local bike shop and ask for a cardboard box. Bikes are usually delivered to shops in cardboard boxes and most of the shops are happy to give these boxes away free of charge.

A word of warning though, check out the exact details with your airline as they are all different. Vueling offers a miserly 20 kg with no flexibility, and I have heard worrying reports about them, like cyclists booking and paying for additional 'sports carrier equipment' assuming it includes a bicycle only to turn up at the airport and find out they need to pay extra for bicycles.

I have detailed transportation options in chapter 14 of this book.

If you are travelling by train, then be warned that the high-speed trains in Spain (called AVE), insist on boxed up bikes but the other trains accommodate cycles from as little as 3€. The

Spanish long-distance Alsa buses allow boxed or bagged bikes for 10€ per trip. I used one of these buses on the way back from Santiago and found them hassle-free.

You need to dismantle your bike for all of the above. Take off the wheels and remove the quick release spindles as this will stick through the box or the bag sides. Remove your pedals and don't forget to bubble wrap your cogs, gear sets and derailleur. You can't be too careful, the last thing you want as you assemble your bike at the other end is to find any damage. Finally, remove the handlebars and cable tie them to the frame. You are now ready to go and chances are you will have more than enough room to push a sleeping bag and a tent into the box.

Top Tip: Get some duct tape and run it around the box several times. You can't be too careful.

Two of us flew from Valencia and it is also worth pointing out that you need a van, a people carrier or a car with a large boot to accommodate two boxed bikes. Check this out beforehand and make sure your bikes fit. It's a pain in the backside transporting and carrying 25 kg boxes that are over a metre long and nearly a metre high. There is no easy way to carry them and a trolley at the airport is a must. Unfortunately they don´t have trolleys at train stations and bus stations. It must also be a nightmare for the baggage handlers as it takes two people to move those boxes from A to B.

Valencia Airport

There were trolleys at Valencia Airport, so we assumed there would be no dramas. We pulled up outside departures and secured a trolley which was just metres away. Happy days, we thought as we put the two boxed up bikes flat on the trolley.

Unfortunately, it wouldn't fit through the sliding doors that led into the airport terminal. We stood the boxes on end and they still wouldn't fit and as a queue built up behind us, we were forced to unload the boxes and carry the 50km through manually. When we went back for the trolley, someone had taken it.

We did manage to find another one and loaded them back up for the two hundred metre push to the Ryanair check-in counter.

Once again, the boxes on the trolley wouldn't fit through the roped off channel that ushers the traveller east, west, east, west, east, west, and finally north and south before you hokey pokey, and turn around until eventually you reach the check-in gate.

The boxes were weighed and we were told to take them to a specified area in another part of the building. We found another trolley (the second one had vanished into thin air) and a nice young woman accompanied us to a lift where the boxed up bikes and trolley wouldn't fit. This was getting ridiculous. Nevertheless, we managed to fit the two boxes in without the trolley and she pressed a button and they were on their way to a higher level where she assured us the luggage handlers would collect them.

I shook my head and couldn't help myself, "wouldn't it be easier for everyone if the bikes weren't in boxes?"

I didn't have to explain myself; she knew exactly what I meant. "Of course it would," she said, "the baggage men hate these boxes, they are heavy and bulky and difficult to manoeuvre."

"Then why don't they change the rules?"

"I don't know," she said.

We said goodbye to Nicole. I wondered if we were ever going to see the bikes again, but it was pointless worrying about it and we decided to hit the bar.

At this point, reality set in. We had managed to get our adventure this far and all being well, a few hours later we would meet our bikes in Bordeaux and it was game on.

"What would you like to drink Caroline?"

"Mine's a wine," she replied.

Our hotel in Bordeaux was only two hundred metres from the airport, so getting a wee bit inebriated wasn't a big issue. We were excited, we were on our way and we celebrated with a few drinks. We'd take a trolley at the other end and push the boxed bikes to the hotel. We had it all planned. We´d assemble them in the morning and nothing could go wrong.

The flight was pleasant enough and we managed to squeeze in another couple of drinks, arriving in

Bordeaux just after 11 pm, slightly merry and full of the joys of our forthcoming adventure.

We managed to find a trolley and loaded the boxes onto it. You guessed it; we couldn't get out the bloody doors again. We thought about assembling the bikes and cycling to the hotel but thought better of it and while Caroline stood guard over the trolley, I wrestled the two boxes outside. We loaded the bikes back onto the trolley and looked for the sign to our hotel. It was an airport hotel, 'two minutes from the airport,' their website said and I assumed it would be easy enough to find, because surely it would be sign posted.

No such luck.

We asked a taxi driver where the Comfort Hotel Merignac was and he shrugged his shoulders. A taxi driver at Bordeaux Airport who didn't know where a Bordeaux Airport hotel was?

I figured that because it was so close and he wasn't going to get a fare, he didn't want to help. We asked someone who looked like a car park attendant and he didn't seem to know either. Eventually, another taxi driver came over and said he had a seven-seater that could take the bikes and he would take us there.

"But it's two minutes away," I said, "just tell me where it is and I'll walk."

"Twenty-five euros," he said, "good price."

"Robbing bastard price," I muttered under my breath, but by now it had started to rain and we were hungry and thirsty.

We paid him 25€ and 45 seconds later we were at the hotel. I resisted the urge to punch him as he smiled when I handed over the money.

"Forget it, Ken," Caroline said, "let's check in and get something to eat."

It looked promising as we walked into the reception area. There was a bar to the right and after a minute or two, a man walked up to us and checked us in. We asked until what time they served food. He told us the kitchen closed at 8 pm. No way! An airport hotel with no food.

Caroline looked at the bar, which was all lit up with soft lights. "It looks like beer and crisps," she announced.

"That will have to do until the morning," I said.

"The bar is closed," the man said.

The bar didn't look closed to me as there were glasses on the counter and the hatch was open. It looked ready for action. We established that the receptionist was also the barman and the night watchman, on duty until seven the following morning. He had the keys to the bar and there was no earthly reason why he couldn't give us a drink but he flatly refused. He told us there was another hotel bar two minutes away. We could get food and drink there he said.

We dumped the bikes in a side room and our luggage in our rather dingy rooms and headed out. We reached the hotel he had mentioned, ordered drinks and picked up the plastic-coated menu, which had a decent selection of burgers, chicken and steaks and my mouth began to water.

But not for long. One of the waitresses had noticed us looking at the menu.

"Sorry, no food, kitchen closed."

This was getting annoying. This is an airport and flights land at Bordeaux airport twenty-four hours a day.

What happened next was a scene reminiscent of Michael Douglas's epic movie, Falling Down. You may remember the scene in the burger bar when he wanted breakfast and was told the breakfast menu finished at 10.30 am. As the camera panned to his wristwatch, we saw it was 10.31. Despite Michael's attempt at reasoning with the staff, they flatly refused to serve him the breakfast menu which resulted in him pulling a gun on the manager.

We ordered another round of drinks.

"The bar is closed."

What? We'd been there 30 minutes and we hadn't heard anybody say the bar was closed.

I asked her what time the bar closed.

"12.30," she replied.

I looked at my watch. It was 12.32.

I turned on the charm. What was two minutes?

She wouldn't have it; her face was like stone. She was a young girl of no more than 20 who was obviously on the late shift and just wanted to get home. I was furious. I asked her why she didn't announce that the bar was closing. That was just a British thing, she said.

So the moral of the story is don't stay in any of the Bordeaux airport hotels. They are expensive, poor value for money, the staff are miserable, they don't like to work and haven't got any concept that an airport runs 24 hours a day.

The hotels are in the middle of an industrial estate and are poorly decorated, shabby and in a nutshell… miserable.

If you do fly into Bordeaux to start your Camino, get a day flight, cycle out of Bordeaux and look for accommodation along your route.

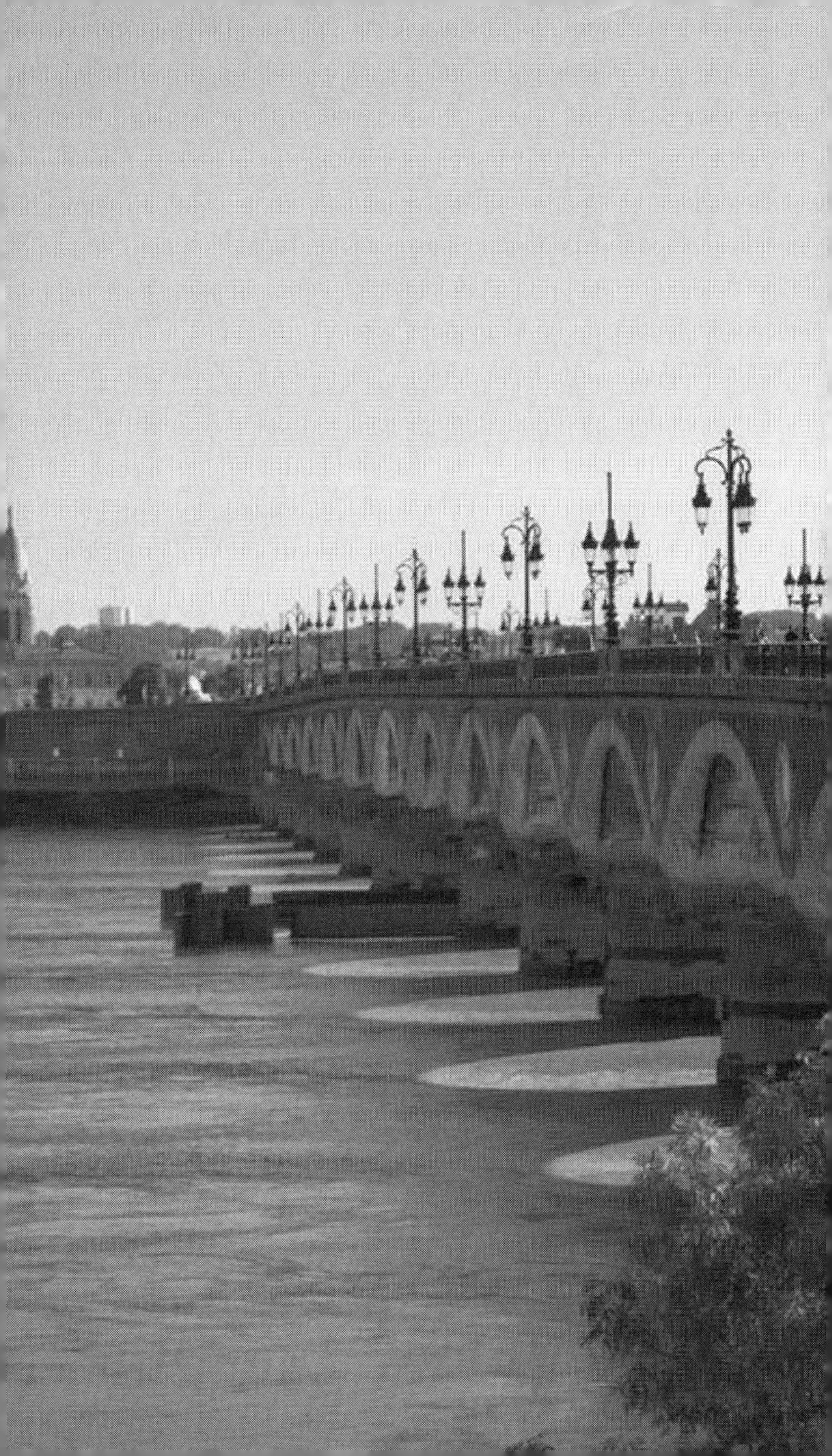

Day One

Bordeaux to Salles

A Gentle Introduction

The following day we put our bikes together, and the adventure was on.
We were heading west towards the Atlantic coast, to a place called Salles, 42 km away and we decided to use Google Maps on a smartphone for directions. We clicked on the bicycle icon so that the app took us onto the cycle paths and avoided roads wherever possible. A bit of advice here - after a few days of using Google Maps, I realised it was good but not infallible. It got us lost a few times and, in France especially, new cycle paths are regularly under construction. You therefore have to be aware and take note of the roads, towns and villages towards which you are heading. That

way, when the app goes wrong, you are still able to head onto the right road.

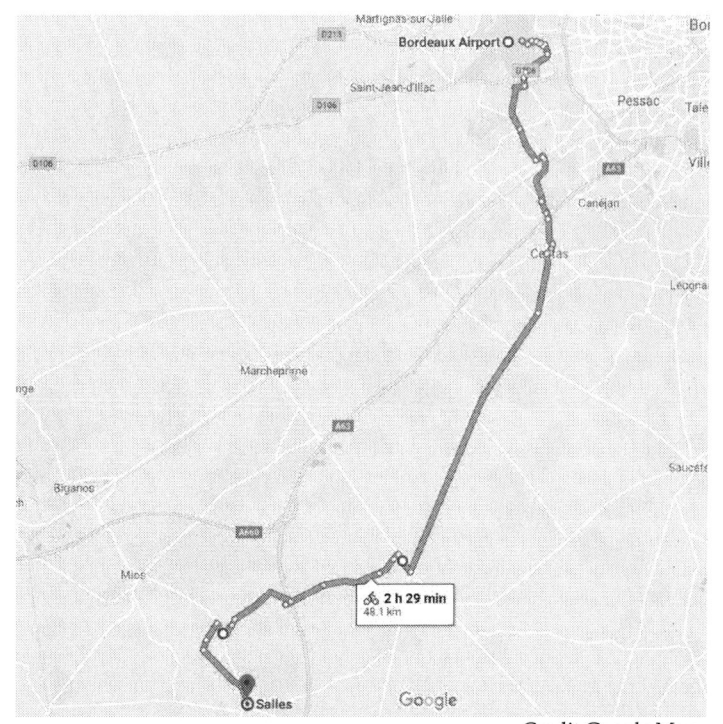

Credit Google Maps

When we left the industrial estate at Bordeaux airport it tried make us go in circles, but because we knew we were looking for the D106 in the direction of Bordeaux Zoo we were able to find the road quite easily because the Zoo was well signposted. Before long, we left Bordeaux behind and after a few cycle paths we were on the D214 riding towards the town of Cestas.

The D214 took us onto the D1010 in the direction of La Barp. The D-roads in France are a cyclist's dream, with good surfaces and the road to Salles was as almost perfectly flat. Our entire elevation for the day was only 121 m.

There were few cars on the road considering it was a Saturday morning and although the scenery was quite bland, we enjoyed the long, straight, tree-lined roads. You have Napoleon to thank for those tree-lined roads that shelter you from the heat of the sun. He had them planted in the early 1800s to protect his marching Grande Armee from the hot summer sun.

We were in no hurry but made good time as we took it easy, averaging around 16 km per hour. We stopped for a couple of beers and lunch on the outskirts of Le Barp and stayed for nearly two hours and got talking to a table of locals. I was surprised but pleased that one of the men was Spanish and we were able to hold a conversation with him. He told us he lived there and that there were a lot of Spanish speaking people in the village, which surprised me because we were still 200 km from the Spanish border. He was quick to tell me that he isn´t Spanish, but Basque and reminded me that we were very close to the French Basque country. He said the Basque people had inhabited the foothills of the Pyrenees Mountains and parts of Southern France for thousands of years.

"We are the oldest surviving ethnic group in Europe," he told me proudly.

I studied Basque history when I wrote the book, 'The Survivor,' the story of Felipe Albero Gomez.

Felipe fought for both sides in the Spanish Civil War and also for the Spanish Blue Division in WWII and he was proud of the fact that he managed to make it through both wars without ever firing one shot. His son is my next-door neighbour and I´m proud to have written the true story of such a soft-hearted gentleman. One of the chapters discusses the bombing of Guernica in the Basque Country. The Basque people have suffered greatly over the centuries and particularly during the Spanish Civil War because Franco and his fascist party wanted to rid Spain of the Basque culture. He banned their language, they lost all political autonomy and economic rights and many were imprisoned or killed. In 1937 Franco ordered the Germans to bomb the market town of Guernica on market day when trading was in full flow.

For those of you interested in the Spanish Civil War and the bombing of Guernica, I quote a few paragraphs from the book below. It's available on Amazon.

"As the first wave of Heinkel bombers flew above their heads towards Guernica, the republican soldiers who were stationed on a hill overlooking Guernica fell silent. It was no more than a few seconds before the dull thuds resonated through the soles of their boots and the dust started to rise from the valley several kilometres in the distance. The soldiers took cover in a small copse at the side of the road as plane after plane flew overhead. They watched as the scene unfolded below them.

Messerschmitts followed the Heinkels and they did not have to wait long to see what their role was in the operation. They flew in random formation around the periphery of the town while firing off bursts of machine-gun fire in the surrounding fields and roads. The terrified refugees and villagers looked like long lines of worker ants."

At this point, Felipe stopped and took time to tell us that an American journalist wrote about the bombing in a foreign newspaper. He had managed to interview some of the survivors and one of the soldiers on the hill. The newspaperman had visited the Marinelarena some days before and met with both Josepe and Alain. He told me never to forget the name of a German called Von Richthofen, for he was the bastard who had orchestrated the massacre.

"The pilots showed no mercy and no respect for age or gender. Their targets had no guns, no defence and no chance. If the pilots missed their intended targets the first time around, they simply banked their planes around and came again. Some had made it into a large wooded area, but the Messerschmitt pilots strafed the area time after time before a sizeable incendiary bomb dropped from a Heinkel scored a direct hit. The heat from the explosion incinerated the entire area and it erupted into a massive fireball. A new noise now; a shrill screaming whistle. The soldiers realised the sound was coming from the bombs as they fell to earth. What was the purpose? No. He shook his head. Surely the whistle was just a trick of the wind, an accident, a natural result of poor aerodynamics.

What were those poor people going through down there?

Josepe and Alain were too old to run. They watched the panicking masses in the street and decided to stay put and say a few prayers to the Almighty. They moved inside with the old lady Marinelarena and Josepe looked at the thick wooden beams and centuries-old stonework that surrounded them. The old lady caught the look. "You are right Josepe; it will take a big bomb to bring this lot down. We are safe here, the good Lord will see over us."

The whistling sound was getting louder now as the three of them cowered under the solid oak table that ran the length of the bar. Josepe covered his ears as Alain shouted something to him that was by now barely audible. The phosphorus bomb sliced through the terracotta tile roof and vaporised everything and everyone inside the bar of Marinelarena as the four walls blew out over, reducing the ancient house to a pile of dust and rubble."

Pepe wiped at a tear and I could almost sense what it must have been like in that Marinelarena.

"And still the German planes bombed and bombed and bombed again for three hours and the Messerschmitts shot at soldiers and refugees, women and fleeing, frightened children, the injured and the dying, cattle, sheep, cats and dogs

and pigs. They shot at anything that moved and those who no longer could, who lay in streets or fields incapacitated and injured with missing limbs or shattered bones.
And then it was silent."

We said goodbye to our Basque friend and his French drinking partners and headed west towards the Route d'Argiles down a small street called the Chemin de Tutou. It took us into a forest and we followed the Google cycle app as it spoke instructions every few hundred metres. It's worth pointing out that there is an alternative route to Salles, via the D1010 and then the D108, but we much preferred the mystery of the forest.
We had booked an Airbnb property on the outskirts of Salles, 2 km from the village, in the heart of the forest. An hour or so from our destination, we typed the exact address into Google Maps.
It was a 12 km ride from La Barp and the app took us right to the door. The small cottage was in the owner's garden. Bernadette is an elderly lady who lives in the main house on her own. She greeted us with mint tea and we spent a little time with her speaking mostly in Spanish, but Caroline drifted into her university French from time to time. Bernadette showed us the small cottage which had two single beds downstairs and a double bed upstairs. As Caroline booked all of the accommodation and being the only girl, the rule

was that she took the best bed, so she claimed the upstairs mezzanine section of the house.

It had been some years since I last camped and was eager to try out my new, one-man tent, so I pitched it at the side of the cottage. The lads who were due in later that evening could have the two single beds.

Each member of our group carried a tent and a sleeping bag on the back of our bike. Even if you are not camping, I would still recommend you take these items as part of your emergency action plan. If we had to set up camp by the side of the road, we knew we could survive whatever nature threw at us. Remember, albergues get full, campsites are few and far between in some places and hotels and guest houses can get booked up many days in advance. There are some great lightweight sleeping bags that weigh less than half a kilo. Tents these days weigh next to nothing and there are dozens of great products on Amazon including the waterproof, two in one combination, the Bivvy Bag, if you want to travel super light.

We met one young couple on the Camino the following week, who had walked 32 km that day and intended to lay their heads in the albergue where we were staying. It was full, and the girl was quite distressed when she heard the next resting spot was more than 10 km away. I had a word with the owner who said they were welcome to camp wherever they could find a spot. As long as they were eating and drinking there,

there would be no charge. They could use the toilets and showers too. The only problem was they didn't have any tents or sleeping bags. We had a bed for the night, so we offered them our tents and sleeping bags and they took us up on the offer. It's worth bearing in mind that most albergue owners are happy to allow camping on their land. They want to sell food and beer, that's where they make their money. Make it a golden rule always to carry something you can sleep in, an insurance policy if you like. That way you can enjoy the day worry-free.

Bernadette showed us the small swimming pool and said that we were welcome to use it, though mentioned that the water was freezing and none of her grandchildren had braved the pool that year. For me it was no problem, I live ten metres from the Mediterranean Sea and swim all year round. So we unpacked and I took a little dip while Caroline took a shower and freshened herself up. She wasn't quite bold enough to take a dip.
We took a phone message from Dave and Gary, who said they had landed in Bordeaux and were outside the airport putting their bikes together. They estimated that they would be there in three hours. Great, we would soon be a complete group. Caroline and I headed for town and after shopping for dinner, enjoyed a couple of drinks at a local bar and cycled back to the cottage to prepare for the lads' arrival.

Gary and Dave had cycled the D1010, D108 road and I met them at the edge of town. We hugged like the long-lost friends we were and it was a very special moment knowing that we could finally put all those months of planning and training into practice. I had two ice-cold bottles of beer for them as they pulled into a bus stop just outside the village and we toasted their health and our adventure that was about to begin.

Only 960 km to go.

We drank enough beer and wine to sink a battleship that night, as we enjoyed the finest French fillet steak for dinner. Although Caroline had met Dave on our training camp in Spain, she had never met Gary, but within an hour of meeting him, they gelled like best buddies.

We drank into the early hours of the morning and played cards and we knew tomorrow was going to be a late start.

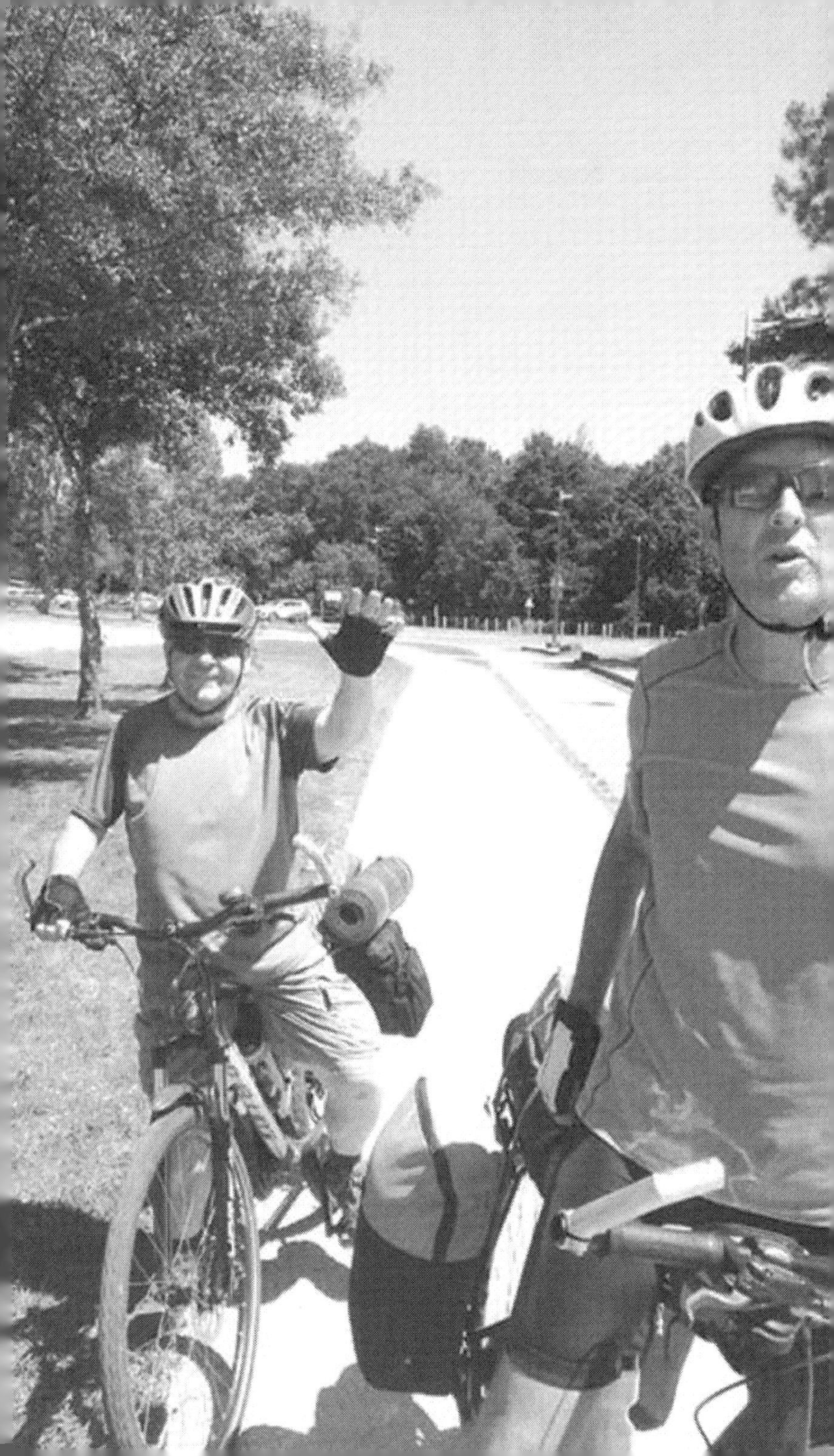

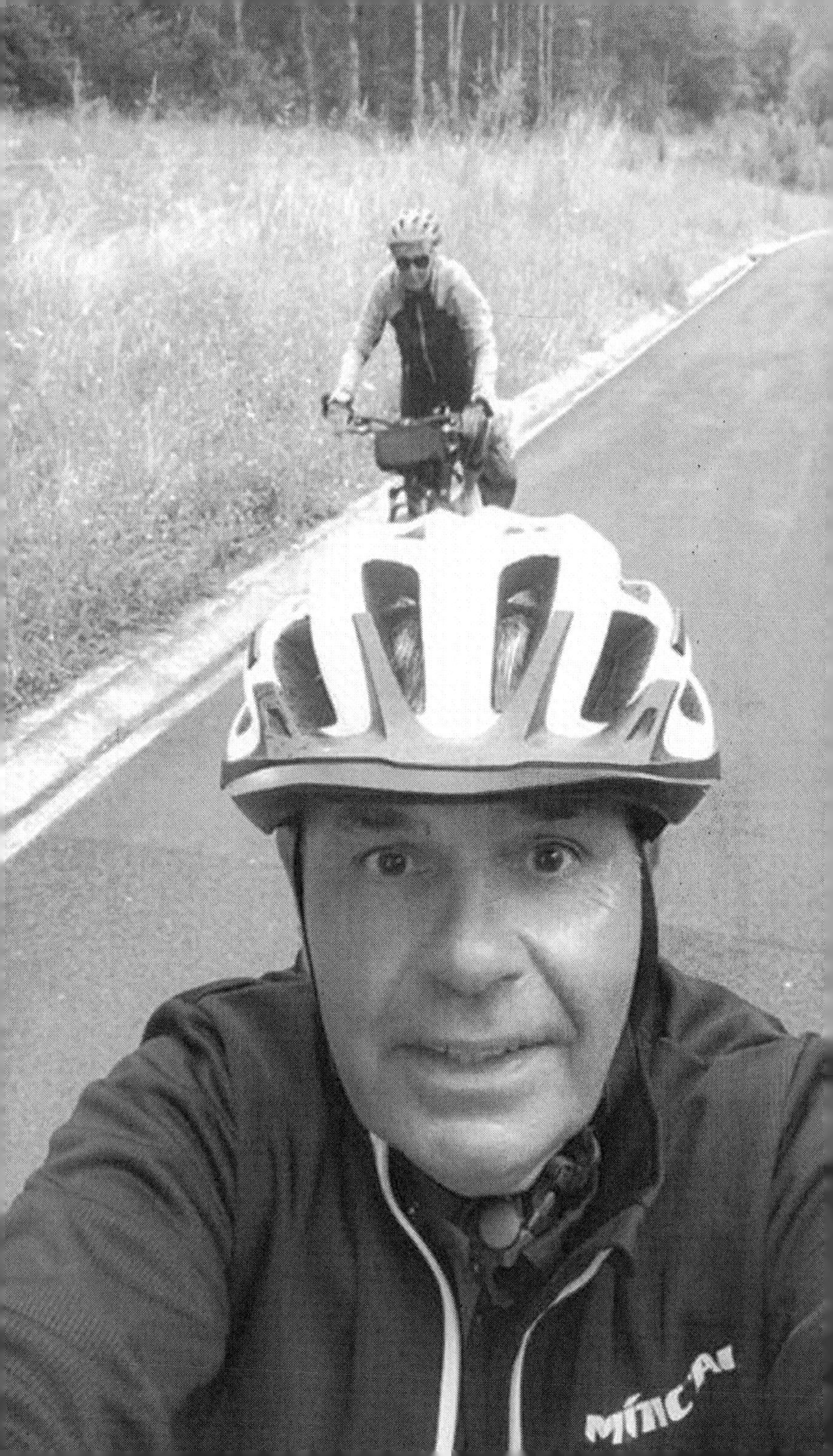

Day Two

Salles to Mimizan Plage

For the Love of French Cycle Paths

We were indeed a little worse for wear the next morning. It seemed like a good idea at the time but at around 9.30 am when we left, the sun was beginning to tease us a little. We had the small matter of a 76 km ride to face though thankfully, according to Google Maps, it was relatively flat. I must point out at this point that although every day we planned our route on Google Maps, the kilometres at the end of the day were always more than what the route map stated. It varied between 10 and 15%. For example, when we arrived at our destination this day, the distance according to Map my Ride and the Relive App was 82 km.

We cycled a couple of kilometres into Salles and although it was Sunday, we managed to find a French patisserie that was open and ordered sandwiches and plenty of coffee. Be wary of Sundays when cycling long-distance, very few shops are open.

Top Tip: Always carry extra food in your panniers and make sure you have plenty of water. Carry cereal bars and chocolate, nuts and dried fruit.

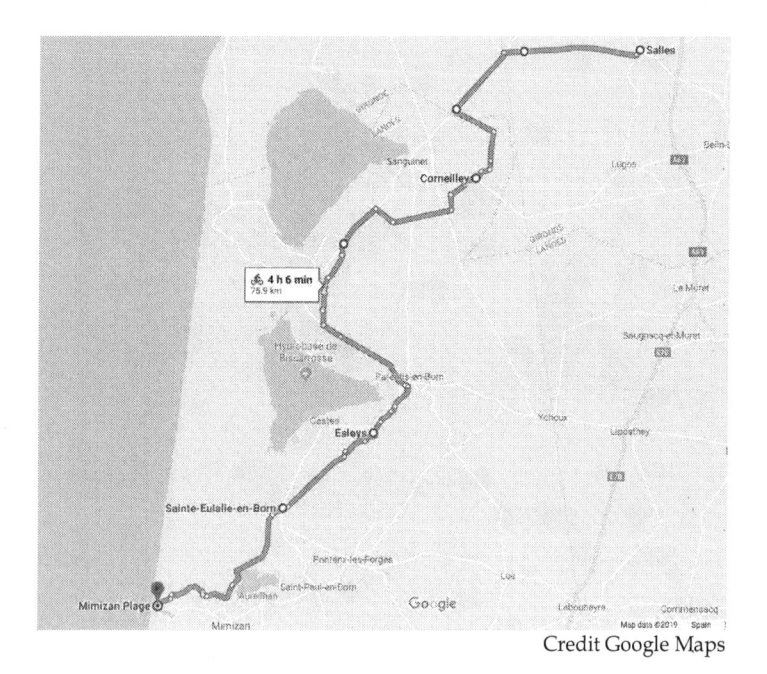

Credit Google Maps

Later that day, we would cycle through villages and towns with no sign of life. The cafés, bars and shops were all closed. It was just as well we had taken on fuel when we had the chance and pushed a few bits and pieces in our kit.

Google Maps took us out of the village and onto the Route de Minoy, mostly on cycle paths that ran next to the D108E3 in the direction of Bilos.

Note: There is a good campsite at Bilos.

It was 16 km to Corneilley and much of the route took us through a forested area. By now, the hangovers were just about beginning to lift, but we were desperate for coffee. We were out of luck. Corneilley was closed and not even a gas station was open so we put our heads down and rode towards Parentis en Born on the D46, and once again we had cycle paths most of the way. In Parentis en Born everything was also closed-up. It was lunchtime, but there were no signs of anywhere to have lunch, so we headed on towards Sainte Eulalie as we spotted the signs for the enormous lake of Hydrobase de Biscarosse.

It was easy cycling and we were all becoming big fans of the French cycle paths. Although it was hot and we hadn't found anywhere to eat, it certainly wasn't unpleasant. However, as lunchtime passed without decent food and the hangover from the night before decided to have a second bite at us, fatigue eventually kicked in. It was now approaching 4 pm and we were all beginning to struggle. The thought of a large beer and a hot sandwich or a burger was never far away from my thoughts. We took a small detour towards Gastes where the vibe changed and suddenly there seemed to be more people around; families with small children out for the day and tourists too. We noticed a sign for a windsurf school and a jet ski centre and then wouldn't you know it, as we skirted the lake and cycled for another few kilometres, just up ahead, an open bar with a huge outside terrace and people sitting outside drinking cold beers and eating ice cream, sandwiches and pizza.

It was like a mirage in the desert; only this was real. I parked the bike and Gary and Dave rolled up beside me.

"Beer?" I asked.

Now, while I love Dave like a brother, there is one thing that not only pisses me off about him, but I can't even begin to work it out. Dave takes indecisiveness to a whole new level.

Gary said a cold beer would go down nicely, but Dave looked at me blankly.

I started walking towards the bar, "what do you want fella?"

"Dunno."

We had been cycling all day and we had been drinking warm water for 3 hours, but now, only 16 or 17 kilometres from our eventual destination we had found a bar.

I'd been dreaming about a beer since the lunchtime we never had.

"Dunno," he repeated, "I'll come and see what they've got."

"Dave, it's a bar," I said. "They have everything, beer, cider, Coca-Cola, Fanta Orange, Fanta Lemon, 7Up, fresh orange juice, fresh pineapple and ice cream. They even have ice-cold bottles of water. What do you want man?"

He shrugged his shoulders and just as I was about to give up on him and order anyway, Gary noticed Caroline was missing. Dave said she had been right behind us a kilometre back.

"She can't be lost," I said, "it's been a straight cycle path for 8 km."

Dave decided to jump on his bike to try and find her, (while he made his mind up about what he wanted to drink.)

I tried to call her, but she didn't answer. I looked longingly at the bar as I palmed the flies from my lips and fought the urge to smack the man ten metres from me who had just taken an enormous mouthful of beer from his glass.

Dave returned five minutes later. No Caroline.

I desperately wanted to order a beer, but it just wouldn't be right. She could be lying in a ditch at the side of the road somewhere. I rang her again and this time she answered. Despite following a straight path for 8 km, there had been a right turn 500 m back and because she couldn't see us, assumed we had turned right. Work that one out.

She rolled up five minutes later.

At last, it was time to order. "Caroline?"

"Oh a beer I think," she said.

"Dave?"

"Dunno."

We were thirsty and starving but decided not to eat that late in the day. The apartment Caroline had booked for that evening had a BBQ and Mimizan Beach, a big tourist destination, was only an hour away so we took a chance that there would be a supermarket open and we could prepare a feast fit for a king.

Those last kilometres into Mimizan were torture.

Top Tip: Do not drink two pints of beer when you still have 16 km to cycle.

It was relatively flat for 10 km but as we approached Mimizan, someone decided to throw in some hills. We were on a cycle path in the heart of a large forest and it was up and down, up and down. By the time we reached Mimizan, I was ready to throw up.

Once again, we entered in the exact address of our apartment into Google Maps and it took us right to the door, in an elegant street just a minute from the town centre. Caroline rang our host and he was there within ten minutes. Airbnb had come good again.

Caroline had booked the first two properties before we left home and I have to say she did a fine job.

The apartment was spotless and had three bedrooms for less than 100€ for the night. The bonus was the stone built-in BBQ with a huge dining table outside, and we took a quick shower and headed for town to find a supermarket and a bar.

While Mimizan looks quite a modern town, it has been around for centuries. The Aquitaine duchy, sprawling out from the Loire to the Pyrenees was formed in the 11th century. For the next seven centuries, pilgrims came from all over Europe, crossing the Landes in the Nouvelle Aquitaine region on their pilgrimage to Santiago de Compostela.

The region in an around Mimizan had recognised resting stops, places of worship and castles. There were hospitals erected by the Knights of St. John of Jerusalem and Mimizan originally known as a Sauveté, a sacred refuge created by the church for the protection of the weak.

The railway arrived in Mimizan in the early 1900s and led to a rapid expansion of the town. Empress Eugenie extolled the benefits of the sea air and the Atlantic Ocean in which she swam regularly, all adding to the appeal of the town.

Mimizan welcomed numerous famous people during the interwar period, and Coco Chanel came here to relax. She had a holiday villa on Mimizan Plage. Charlie Chaplin and Salvador Dalí were regular visitors too and Winston Churchill was said to have visited the area and produced 20 paintings on the banks of Lake Aureilhan.

We sat outside a small bar in the evening sunshine and took in the atmosphere. The area was clearly very popular with holidaymakers. It was beautiful and stylish with traditional bars and stores as well as designer shops around a large town square. We asked about a supermarket and thankfully they told us a small supermarket was open at the far end of town. The boys had decided to go swimming in the Atlantic and Caroline and I wandered up to the supermarket to get some grub.

We met up with the boys as we came from the supermarket. Unfortunately, they didn't get to swim as the current was too strong and there were notices on the beach prohibiting swimming.

We returned to our apartment, fired up the barbeque and settled in for the evening. We had sausages and spicy chicken, pancetta, peppers and roast potatoes. We drank a three litre box of wine and put the world to rights.

Dave and I were the last ones standing; Caroline and Gary slipped off to bed around midnight. (Not together, I hasten to add.)

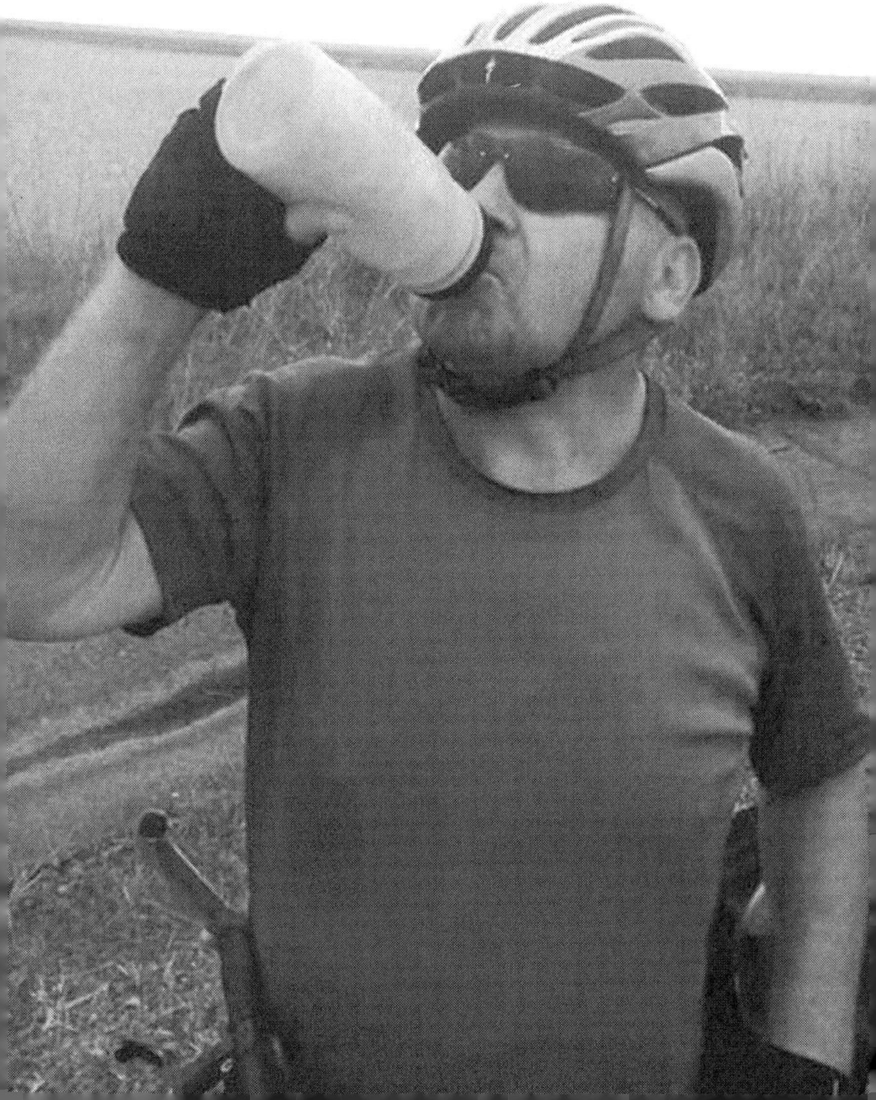

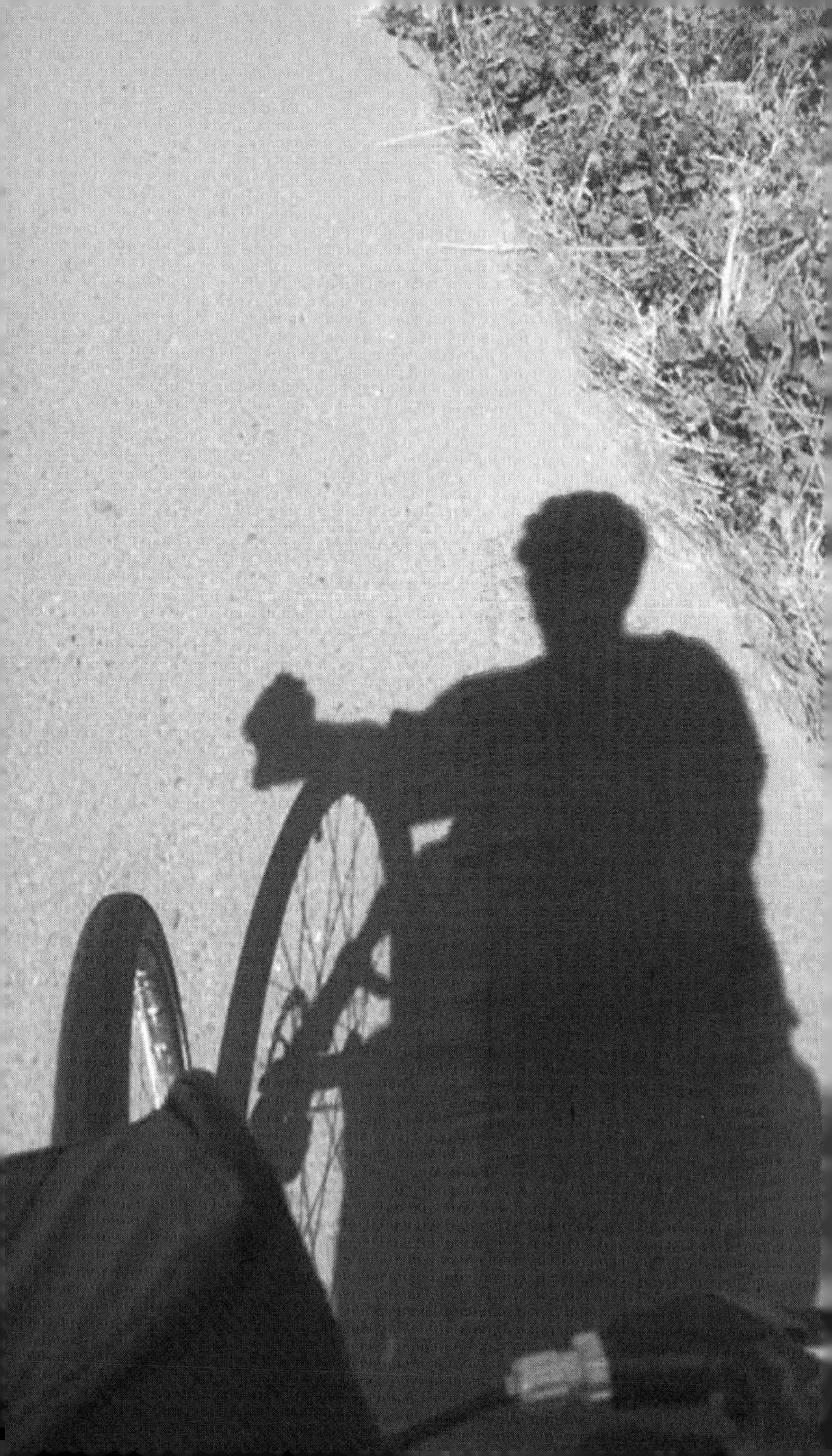

Day Three

Mimizan to Capbreton

Just a perfect day, I'm glad I spent it with you.

After another great night, we were heading for Capbreton. That was the plan anyway and much to Caroline's delight, it would be our first night camping.
I cycled into town just after 8 am, picked up some eggs, bread and jam, had a quick coffee and headed back to the apartment. Caroline and the boys were up by then and preparing the bikes for our 80km ride.
We made scrambled eggs and coffee and had breakfast at the table where we had barbequed the night before. The weather once again looked good and we chilled for another hour and drank more

coffee. Dave looked a little fragile and swore he would never drink as much wine again, especially while on a cycling holiday. I studied the elevation of the ride and told him not to worry. It looked like an easy day, around 300 m elevation with approximately five hours in the saddle.

Credit Google Maps

I once again congratulated Caroline on finding such a great place on Airbnb. This was so easy; it was the first time I had used Airbnb, but I was fast becoming a fan.

Google Maps sent us back towards town and onto a small beach road. We cycled through a couple of urbanisations and then found ourselves on a cycle path that ran alongside the Atlantic Ocean and we looked forward to catching glimpses of the sea along the entire route. We were disappointed though, as the path was always more than 500 m from the ocean, which was hidden by huge dunes.

But that didn't matter because one cycle path led to another and then to another as we trundled through a vast wooded area that shaded us from the sun. Before long, we had clocked up 20 km and weren't even out of breath.

There are no roads to tell you about on this part of the journey because although we did cycle next to a few main roads, we had cycle paths all the way. They were easy to find and we didn't get lost once. The only minor downside of the route was that there were no bars to stop for coffee, but it was so lovely and such easy terrain that we pushed on around 35 km to a place called Saint Girons.

A signpost showed that Saint Girons´ beach was only a kilometre from the cycle path and we debated whether to push on or take the diversion down to the beach.

We decided to give it a go, as it was baking hot and the thought of a swim in the refreshing Atlantic was too much of a temptation.

It was all downhill and we freewheeled towards the ocean and what looked like a one-horse western town appeared in front of us.

There were half a dozen shops on one side of the street and three or four bars on the other and that was it. Some of the shops and the bars were closed and that surprised me because it was midday in June and this looked like a small holiday resort. Judging by the shops, it was also a surfer's paradise. It didn't matter, the bar at the end of the street, just before the beach, was open and we parked the bikes outside and walked in.

I ordered a beer (surprise, surprise) and collapsed into a big soft sofa inside. The rest of the gang decided they wanted more sun and sat outside.

"You need to get some shade," I said, "it's forecast to be even hotter this afternoon."

By now it was 33 degrees; 91 degrees Fahrenheit in old money. They wouldn't have it. The lads were enjoying the sun after the grimness of England and Caroline wanted to top up her tan.

So we sat for an hour or so and nobody wanted to move, because it was absolute paradise.

It was time for a swim, but Gary and Caroline decided against it. Caroline didn't want to change into her bikini and Gary said the Atlantic was notoriously cold and he wasn't going anywhere near it.

Dave and I walked down the street and onto the beach. It was a glorious sight with beautiful white sand as far as the eye could see. It was about 200 m to the ocean and as we neared the water the beach opened up and you could see for miles in both directions. There were probably no more than a dozen people on the beach and just a handful of windsurfers braving the huge waves. There appeared to be more lifeguards than tourists.

We walked towards the water. The last time I had braved the Atlantic surf was in Portugal some years back in August and it was freezing so as we walked in ankle-deep, I prepared for the shock.

But no, I was amazed that it felt about the same temperature as the Med back home.

"It's gorgeous," Dave said.

We had no sooner dived into the surf when a big 4x4 Jeep came speeding along the sand, hooting. The two lifeguards inside were blowing whistles and gesturing at us.

"They're telling us to get out," Dave said.

"It's not going to happen," I replied, "they are going to have to come in here and drag me out."

"Me too," Dave said, "I'm staying put."

We were only waist-deep in the water and even if a great white shark appeared and tried to drag me out to sea, I was reasonably confident that I could still make it back to the shore. After a couple of hours cycling in the heat of the day I could feel my body temperature dropping and it was exhilarating. We were staying where we were for as long as possible.

However, it turned out that the lifeguards weren't throwing us out, they were simply directing us a couple of hundred metres along the beach because at the spot we had gone in there was a fierce rip current which could pull a swimmer out to sea.

We swam to where the lifeguards had directed us and spent another 15 glorious minutes swimming in the Atlantic.

I remember floating on my back and thinking how contented and relaxed I was. It had been an almost perfect morning on the Camino and we had a great afternoon of cycling ahead.

Back on the strip we met up with Gary and Caroline, bought a few provisions at the shop and set off up the hill.

Moilets et Maa was our next scheduled stop where we would hopefully have lunch.

We probably spent a little too long at the beach at Saint Girons as it was after 2 pm by the time we rolled up at Moilets et Maa. Again, there had been cycle paths the whole way, but we were aware that the temperature was creeping ever higher and our water intake was high.

But there was nothing at Moilets et Maa; no bar and no shop or even a fountain to replenish our diminishing water supply so we cycled on for another hour to the next village of Vieux Boucau.

We found a nice bar. It looked promising as there were a couple of tables with people taking lunch and the food looked good. We sat down and ordered some drinks and we managed to make our minds up quite quickly about what we wanted to eat. Probably because it was now after 3 pm and we hadn't eaten anything substantial since breakfast.

"The kitchen is closed," the girl behind the bar said.

We looked at the six people eating at the neighbouring tables. She explained that they were the staff and they were on their designated lunch break. The kitchen would reopen at 6 pm.

This would happen a lot during our journey, and once again, I emphasise the need to carry food and plenty of water with you and take a refuelling stop whenever you can.

There were many occasions when we came across a bar or a café serving food and we thought it was either a little too early, or we'd 'throw in a few more kilometres' before we stopped for breakfast or lunch.

In hindsight, this was a mistake; we should have eaten when we had the opportunity.

Midway through the challenge I spoke to Steve Nash, a pal back home. Steve is a very experienced Camino hiker and he told me to make pit stops whenever we can.

"The same goes for your accommodation in the evenings," he said, "even if you roll up at a nice albergue a couple of hours before your intended stop, if it has food and accommodation then call it a day."

It was great advice. I wish we had listened to him, but of course, it's not until you make those mistakes yourself that you learn from them. You will read about a day in a future chapter when we were caught out to the extent that it could have turned quite serious.

Anyway, at Vieux Boucau we were lucky because there was a sandwich shop two hundred metres away and their kitchen was open all day. We parked and sat in an outside area where they brought us cold drinks and as much food as we wanted. In the end, we opted for chicken and goats cheese salads and they were well worth the money.

We set off an hour later, and again we had cycle paths right into Capbreton. You'll notice I haven't mentioned any road numbers on this day of the challenge and that's because there weren't any. The last few kilometres into Capbreton took us into a forest and onto a cycle path that gave us our first serious bit of climbing that day. Dave was struggling at this point and for the first time I learned that he was only carrying one water bottle on his bike with none in reserve and he had run out more than 10 km back.

It was clear he was severely dehydrated and I also remember how he baked himself at St Girons Plage that morning and again at the sandwich shop. We learned a big lesson that day.

By the time we rolled into Capbreton the temperature had hit 37 degrees and cycling through the middle of town, with no breeze and the heat from the car engines, was the most unpleasant part of the day.

The campsite, Camping La Civelle was easy to find and Google Maps took us right there. We had booked our pitches 24 hours in advance, but they had a lot of space available. Pitching our four single tents cost a total of 25€ for the night. It was cracking value for money as the site had everything we wanted and was five minutes from the beach with a large swimming pool as well. We had a large pitch and those on either side were empty, so we were spoiled for choice.

It was still bloody hot, too hot to pitch tents so Dave and Gary headed for the pool to cool down and surprise, surprise Caroline and I wanted to know where the bar was. Problem solved, I thought, as I spotted a UK registered mobile home with a couple sitting outside, enjoying the last hour of the sun's rays.

I wandered over and asked. They pointed toward some trees and gave me directions. "Three minutes' walk," they said.

There was no time for general chit chat and Caroline and I skipped away, but we were about to get well acquainted with the couple we now know as Diane and Chris Jackson.

Gary and Dave joined us on drink number two and we had already studied the menu and established that the campsite bar was open all evening and that pizza appeared to be their speciality, with a special stone oven on site.

Dave had just about regulated his body temperature and we made a vow to take it easy that evening as we had a big day's cycling the following day with a lot more climbing than we had experienced today.

We pitched our tents and showered, and within the hour we were back in the bar preparing for a relaxing, quiet evening.

Dave described the campsite at Capbreton as the best he has ever visited. When it comes to campsites, the French know how to do it, and of course, in the south of the country, they generally get good weather too.

Camping (despite what Caroline will tell you), is a great way to enjoy the Camino. First of all, you are at one with nature, you see so much more, you feel so much more, you can almost sense how those first pilgrims struggled and suffered when the Camino de Santiago was in its medieval heyday.

Don't get me wrong, the accommodation we had experienced to date had been first class and there's nothing like curling up on a soft mattress at the end of a tough day with a roof over your head. However, pitching a tent in a field and then crawling into the cramped space in the darkness and settling down for the night takes some beating in my book, as does getting up early the next morning as the first birdsong wakes you up to the new day.

With the tents pitched, we headed back to the campsite bar. We noticed that Capbreton town had an abundance of bars and restaurants when we had cycled through it some hours before, but this small campsite bar had everything we needed and it was a unanimous decision to stay put. It had been a long hot day and no one was eager to jump back on a bike and head to town.

Soon after, Diane and Chris joined us and within a couple of hours, our promise to ourselves of a quiet night had disappeared into the French night. To say we gelled with Chris and Diane is an understatement. They are great folks, and we laughed long and hard through the night as we eventually persuaded them to pull their table over to join ours. It had been six weeks since Diane and Chris had spoken to anyone in English and it was clear that they enjoyed the evening as much as we did. They are a couple in their fifties who had quit their jobs to escape the rat race and took off in their mobile home on a year-long holiday, staying a few days here and a few weeks there.

When we told them the purpose of our little adventure is to cycle 1,000 km in two weeks, they couldn't quite believe it.

Diane asked Caroline where we lived, and Caroline told her where we live in Spain.

"Is it near Benidorm?" she asked.

"Thirty minutes away," Caroline replied.

Benidorm is on the list of 'must visit' places for Chris and Diane and the two women spent the evening hatching plans. Dianne eventually announced that, if we manage to complete our challenge, her and Chris will try to make it to Benidorm to meet up with us. That same evening we received a message from one of Caroline's friends, Nicky Chapman, to say she had organised a welcome home party and a fundraiser for the charity in The Church Bar in Albir.

It was a little premature as we had only completed 210 km, but we appreciated the gesture.

Diane was more excited than Caroline, "we'll be at the party," she said, "and if you complete the challenge, we'll contribute to Marie Curie.

By the end of the evening, as they became our best friends and we drank the wine cellar dry, I didn´t doubt that if we managed to make it to Santiago de Compostela in one piece and then back home, that Diane and Chris would indeed keep their promise.

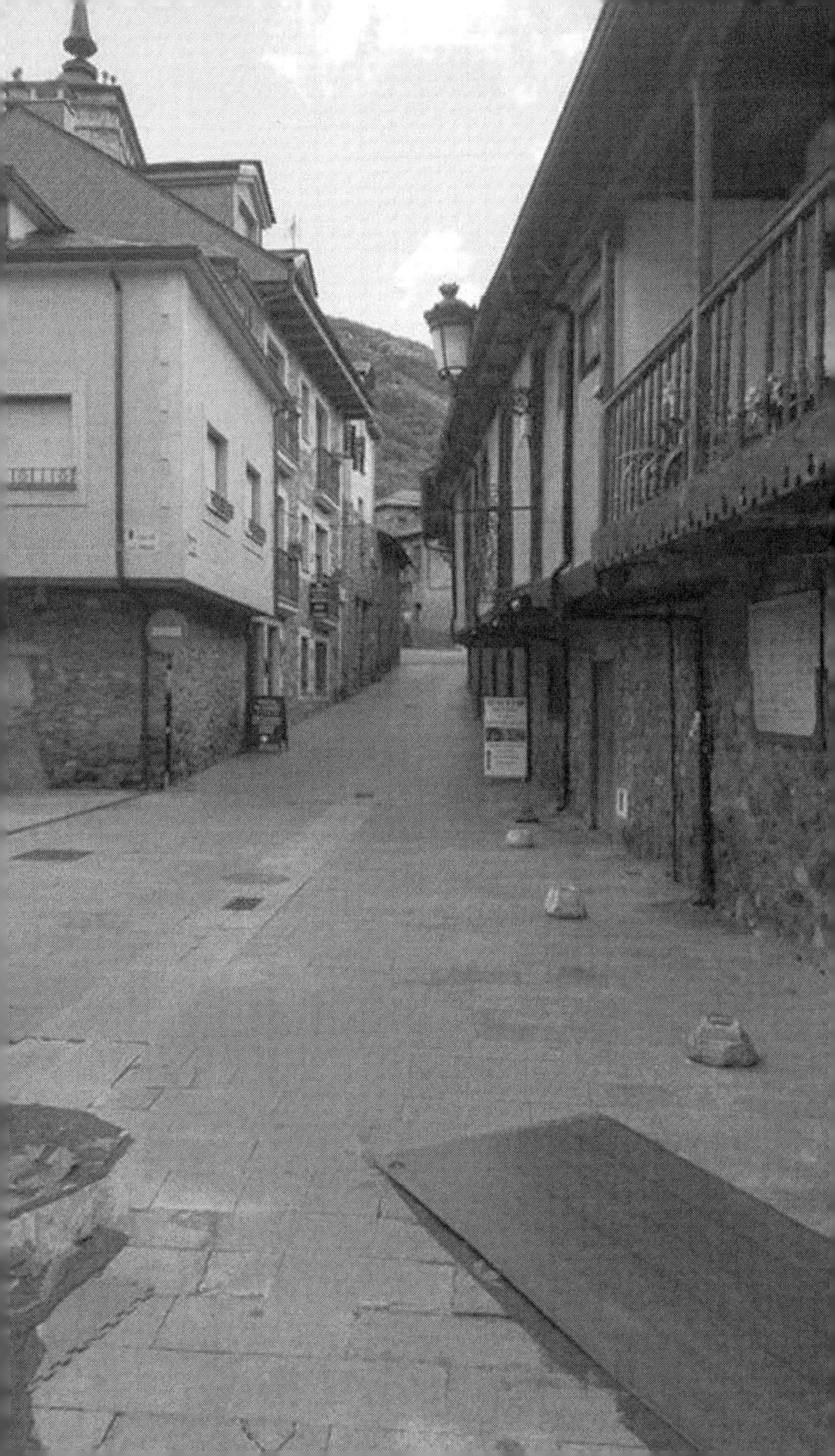

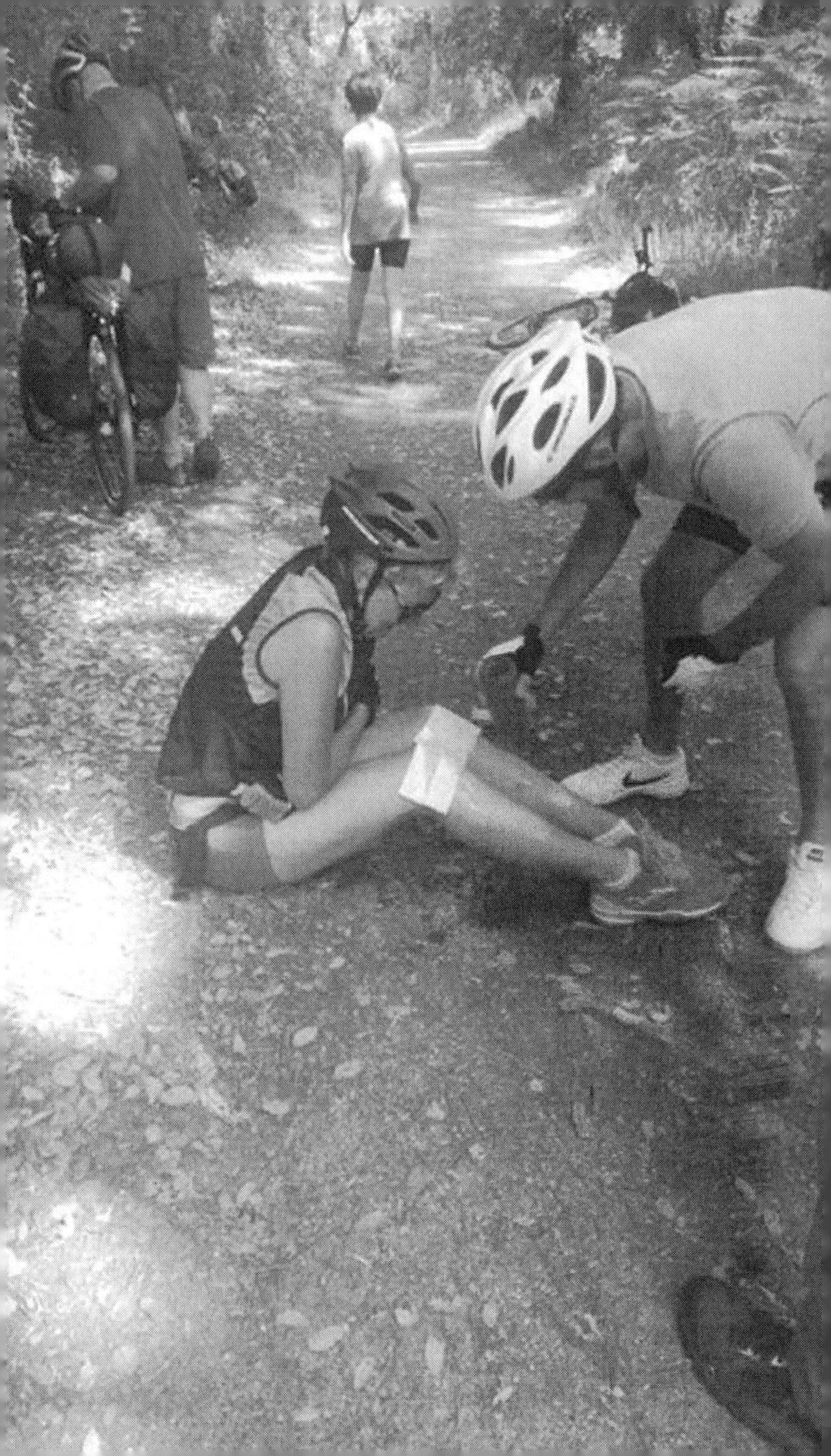

Day Four

Capbreton to Hendaye

The day from Hell

Cycling the Camino de Santiago is much like playing golf. Just when you´ve had the round of your life and you´ve found the secret to the game, the gods conspire against you and deliver a hefty punch in the gut, reminding you that all is not what it seems.

And so, after one of the most pleasant days' cycling I can ever remember, from Mimizan to Capbreton, the gods threw in the day from hell. It started badly and grew progressively worse.

The image below is from the Google Maps App and you can see, I've highlighted the cycle icon. That instructs the map to guide us onto cycle paths wherever possible.

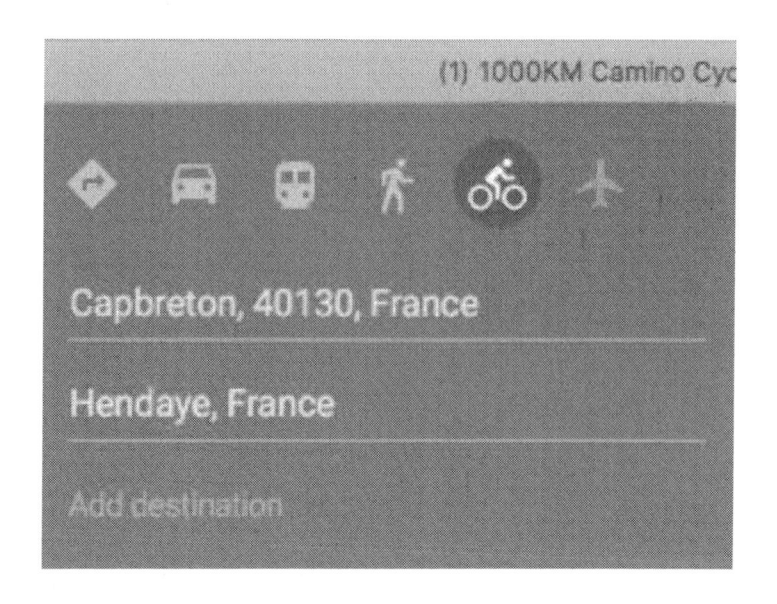

Credit Google Maps

Whenever you start your morning ride, make sure you have highlighted the cycle icon otherwise it defaults onto the car route and sends you on the fastest route available. This includes motorways and toll roads where cycles are not allowed.

We said goodbye to Diane and Chris and set off with mild hangovers but otherwise in high spirits. Unfortunately, the team leader, me, was in such high spirits he forgot to set the cycle icon.

I should have realised after a few kilometres when we hadn't picked up a cycle path that something was wrong. The road was busy and we were in rush hour traffic. We'll reach a cycle path soon, I thought.

After more than 5 km it directed me towards a toll road. No worries I thought, occasionally a cycle path runs next to a motorway for a few kilometres. But no. We got right to the 'take a ticket' sign, there still wasn't a cycle path in sight and the app was telling me to continue straight for 22 km. I knew exactly what had happened and sure enough, when I checked the phone, there was the little car icon smiling back at me.

I reset it, and it took us right back to the campsite; 12 wasted kilometres and just by the gate to the entrance of the site, we joined the cycle path we should have taken an hour ago.

Sadly, it would be a sign of things to come on the road to hell.

The first 20 km were okay, mostly cycle paths and minor roads and for about 3 km we skirted the river Ardour, just before Bayonne.

The landscape then changed, turning rapidly industrial as it took us into the city centre. It was pretty scary; the roads were quite narrow with huge trucks hurtling past us just a couple of metres away. We were due a stop but made the decision to get out of there as quick as possible and headed towards Biarritz.

At this point, the Google Maps chica went silent on me and refused to talk, which sometimes happens if the GPS signal is lost. I pulled over and we looked at the maps and it was clear that for some reason the GPS was not working properly.

Then we started to climb towards Biarritz on major roads and someone turned up the temperature – probably the same gods who had been plotting against us all day. We got lost and went around in circles several times before the Google Maps chica sent us down a huge hill for about 1 km. It was a nice respite from the almost constant climbing that we had endured for the last hour. At the bottom of the hill, she told us to do a U-turn and continue back up the hill we'd just cycled down. By the time we reached the top of the hill, we had run out of water, but we found a bar where we could refill the bottles. At this point, we probably should have stopped, but we were in the middle of an industrial estate and made the collective decision to push on.

The troops were getting restless and there were distinct murmurs of discontent. I could hardly blame them.

Biarritz was a disappointment and not what I expected. We went through the ugly industrial part of town, and we never got to see the beautiful golden sands and beautiful scenery at La Grande Plage that we had heard about because the roads we took were heading south and we just wanted to get out of there.

The GPS took us onto a ring road and eventually we left Biarritz behind as we headed 7 km down the road to a place called Bidart. At last, the GPS took us into a forest with no cars or juggernauts and we did our best to try and chill out while the forest canopy sheltered us from the baking sun.

Sheer bliss, those gods had punished us enough. Surely it would be plain sailing for the rest of the day?

Not so, those invisible little bastards in the sky weren't finished yet, not by a long shot.

Accident number one took place when Caroline stopped in the forest to play with a dog.

"C'mon Caroline, we are way behind schedule."

But no, Caroline hadn't seen her darling pooches for nearly a week and she was missing them. As she picked up a stick to throw for the dog, she uttered the now infamous words "what harm can it do?"

As the stick flew through the air, the dog took off after it, but Fido didn't have far to run because the sharp-pointed stick buried itself into Dave's head.

There was blood everywhere and we were convinced Dave would need stitches. To be fair to Caroline, she was mortified and very concerned for him.

We patched him up, and he didn´t need the hospital.

It was no more than ten minutes later when Calamity Caroline struck again. We were still in the forest with Gary, Dave and me cycling ahead and Caroline about 50 m back. We were travelling at about 15 km/h and as we turned a corner, we saw an old man walking his two dogs. The path was no more than six feet wide and there was nowhere to go, so we stopped while the man apologised and called his dogs to heel.

We were talking to the man and I was making a fuss of his beagle as Calamity turned the corner and despite having owned her bike for over seven months, absent-mindedly forgot where her brake levers were. She smashed into us and catapulted over the handlebars, landing in a heap while cursing us for having the audacity to stop.

I can´t lie; it was funny. She was the first to admit it was karma for splitting Dave's head open.

Fortunately she wasn't too badly hurt, a couple of plasters and a bandage to her knees applied by two passing doctors who were also cycling the Camino.

Later, a sign in the forest told us that we were in the Basque country and suddenly Spain didn't seem so far away. I consoled myself by calculating the kilometres we had ridden so far. I thought ahead to a nice lunch and a beer and tried to block out everything that had happened that day.

We were so glad to get out of that forest, and thankfully both injured parties were well enough to soldier on.

When we got out of the forest, we promptly got lost again.

It was the day from hell.

I was also struggling a bit in the undercarriage department. I was decidedly uncomfortable and couldn't understand it because, for the five years since I started cycling, I have never experienced saddle soreness. And don't forget, we had completed a six-day training camp before the challenge. I had been on the same bike with the same saddle and had been fine. I couldn't work it out; it felt as if someone had taken a piece of sandpaper to the bones of my backside.

Just outside Bidart, we got lost again. The GPS was working fine and the chica couldn't stop talking to me, but she was sending us on a wild goose chase, and it was so hot.

We eventually made it to a glorious beach bar just outside Bidart.

The beauty of your bad experiences on the Camino is that they are quickly forgotten. In the beach bar at Bidart, the beer was ice cold and the goat's cheese salad was to die for. In the cool bar with a nice breeze blowing in from the Atlantic we ate and drank with gusto while we laughed about the trials the gods had put us through that day.

Gary said, "it wasn't that bad, it was a decent run at times."

At this point, you may want to check out the video of our pit stop in Bidart. Join the Facebook group Camino de Santiago Cycle Challenge and go back on the timeline to 18 June 2019. You will see Gary and me discussing the nightmare of a day we had just had. Scroll further down and you will see the aftermath of the accidents as well.

We had 20 km to go before our planned stop in Hendaye. We decided to forego GPS for the day and simply use the roads. It was clear that Google Maps was having a bad day and we just didn't have the time to get lost again.

The D810 was busy at times, not the ideal sort of road to cycle on but we pressed on and were relieved to see the 10 km sign to Hendaye. What we didn't realise was that it was 8 km of climbing, the last thing we needed on the last part of the day from hell.

We arrived in Hendaye exhausted. It was late so we knew we wouldn't have a lot of time to look around. We just wanted to shower, eat and go to bed.

Hendaye is worth exploring though. It's the most south-westerly seaside resort in France and it's steeped in history, being briefly occupied by the Spanish in 1636 during the Franco Spanish Wars.

In 1659, after decades of fighting, the Treaty of the Pyrenees was signed on a fortified island in the river Bidassoa. The island, Ile des Faisans (Pheasant Island), to this day still alternates ownership between France and Spain every six months. How that works, I'll never know. And you thought Gibraltar was complicated!

In the elegant town square there's an open-air market every Wednesday and it's also the location of the stone-carved, 'Great Cross of Hendaye,' with alchemical and occult symbols. It allegedly contains an encrypted message warning of a future global catastrophe. If you like that sort of thing, the church of Saint-Vincent is worth a look too. It was built-in 1598, and largely reconstructed over the centuries following fires and bombardments. The promenade and the seafront are also worth an early evening stroll and keep an eye out for the Chateau of Antoine d' Abbadie, a stunning monument of Gothic Architecture.

The 60 km trip we had planned turned into 82 km, we'd had two accidents and cycled twice through horrendous city traffic.

It was all forgotten as we checked into our apartment and wandered out to find a bar. Hendaye is a beautiful place and what amazed me was how, as a group, we all found humour in the disasters that had hit us that day. Caroline got ridiculed most of the evening as was expected, but she took it all in her stride, like the class act she is, and as the navigator and group leader I also got my fair share of stick.

This is exactly what your Camino Cycle Challenge is all about. Not every day is going to be perfect and there won´t be flat cycle paths with bars every few kilometres. Remember this is a challenge and it's not for everyone. The easiest thing to do on your summer break is to curl up on a beach somewhere hot and read a book, but I don´t think you´re that sort of person because you wouldn´t have bought this book if you were. You're an adventurer and sometimes adventurers have to put up with some shit. Remember, a path with no obstacles probably doesn't lead anywhere worthwhile. I recently read the book of Darroch 'Daz' Tait, the intrepid adventurer and round the world sailor. His book, The World's my Oyster, is stunning, and like this book, it doesn't just tell the reader about the good times, his ventures on the Patagonia ice glaciers or his times diving in the Galapagos. He tells it how it is, that the life of an adventurer isn't always easy and at times it´s even dangerous.

The beautiful thing about our intrepid cycling group was that we were all able to laugh and forget about the bad things that went before. There's nothing worse than a moaner, someone who will talk long and hard into the night and the next day and the next day about all the bad things that happened while conveniently forgetting about the good bits of the day.

My memories of Capbreton to Hendaye will be about the laughs we had in the forest, the three or four kilometres along the banks of the river Ardour and the beautiful lunch at Bidart and that first delicious beer in Hendaye as we ripped the piss out of each other. That is what it's all about, don't let the personas negativas tell you otherwise.

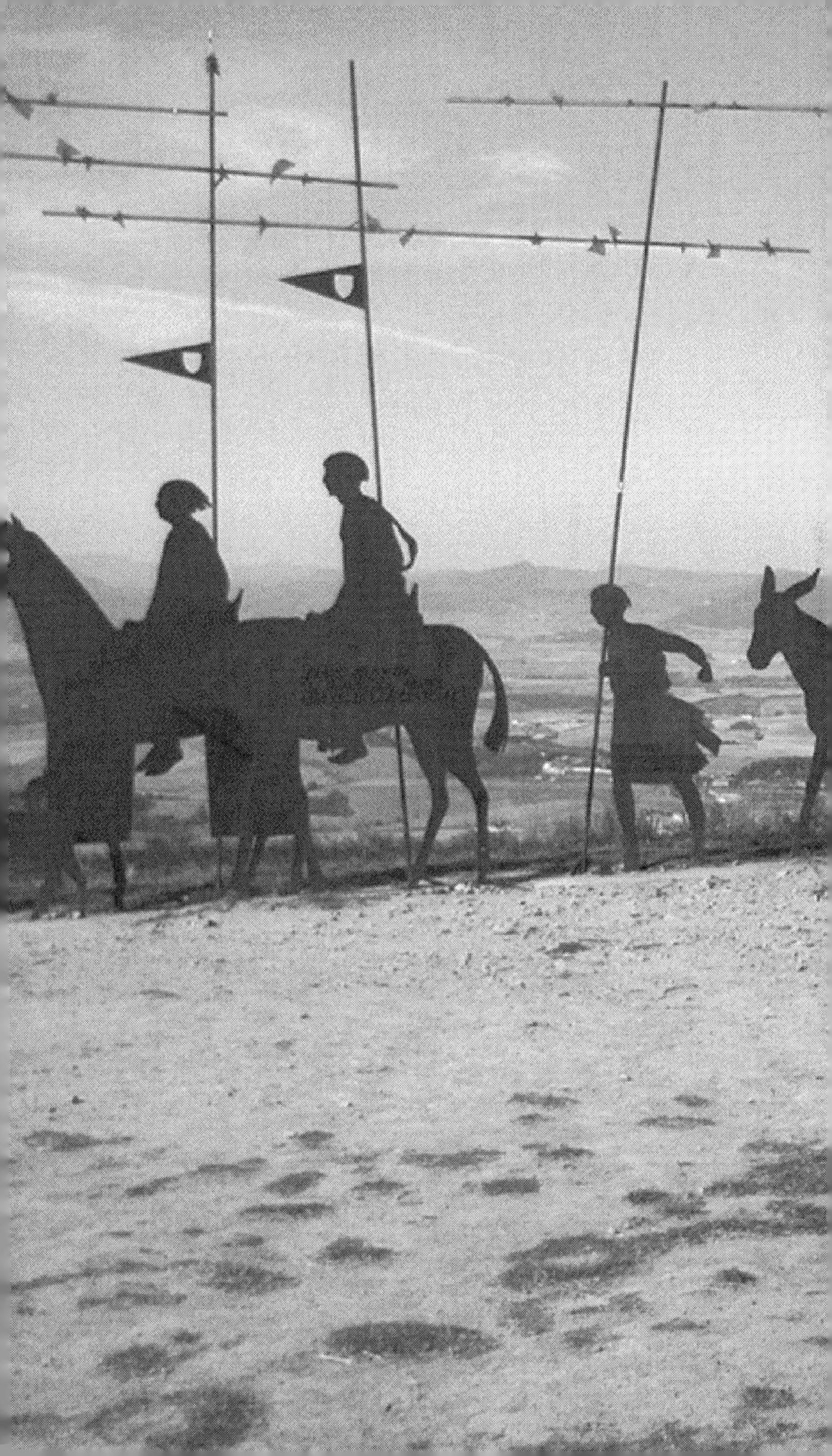

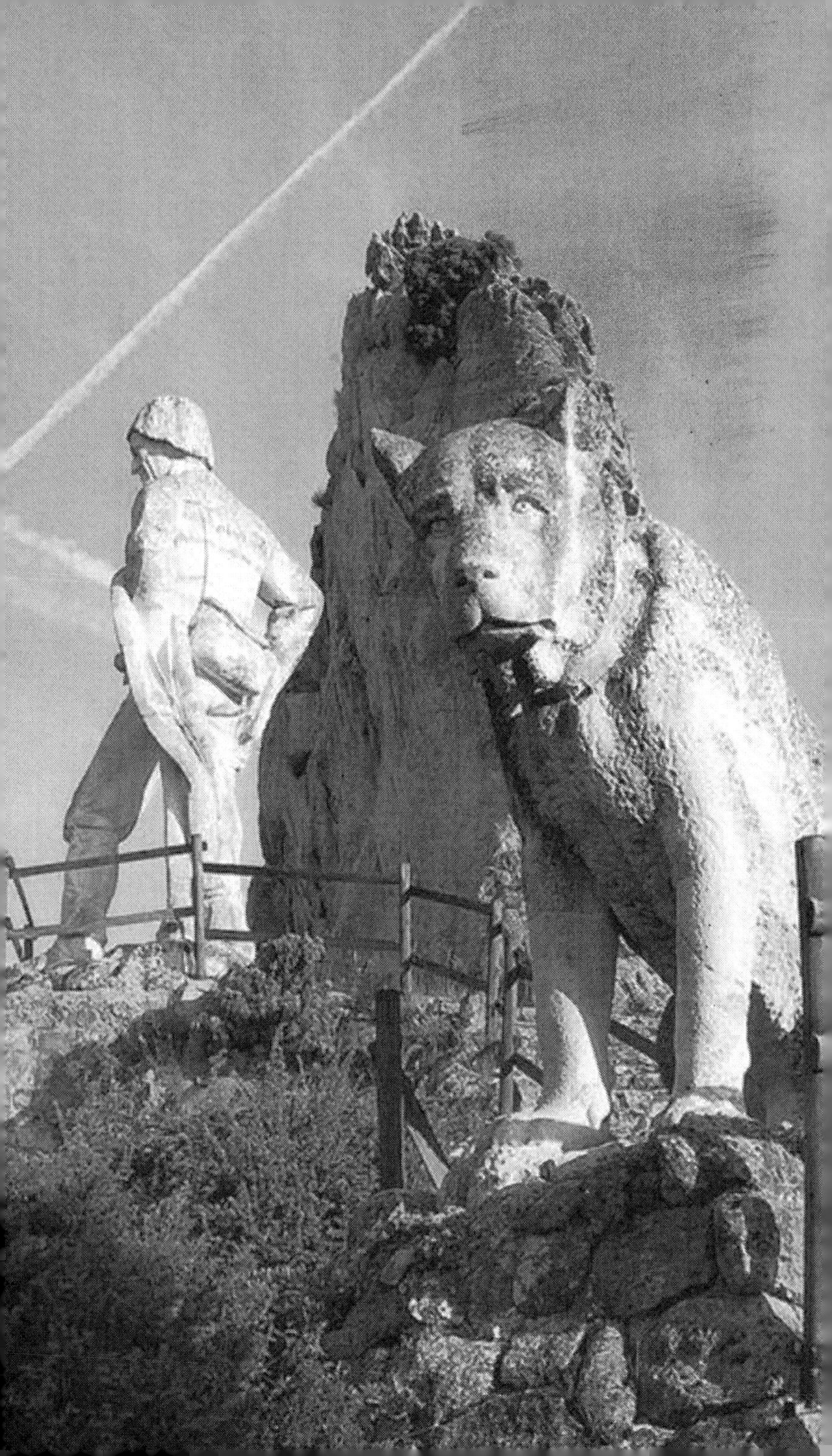

Day Five

Hendaye to Tolosa

A change of direction; two options

In the previous chapter I detailed our route from Capbreton to Hendaye, but this wasn´t the route we had originally planned. We had planned to turn east at Bayonne and head for the traditional starting point of the Camino, at Saint-Jean-Pied-de-Port.

However, at Capbreton we re-evaluated the route and considered the additional kilometres and elevation. Our original goal was always just to complete 1,000 km on the Camino and going to Saint-Jean-Pied-de-Port would add an extra 100 km to the route. We also looked at the additional 1,800 m of elevation from Saint-Jean-Pied-de-Port to Tolosa and we decided to give it a miss.

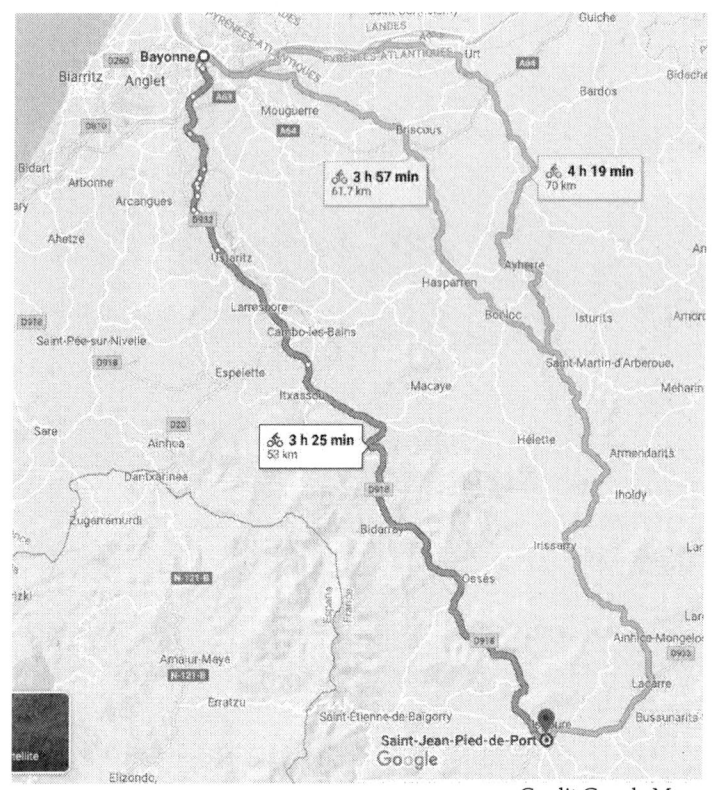

Credit Google Maps

I don´t want to dissuade anybody from travelling to Saint-Jean-Pied-de-Port and starting from there. It is an iconic starting point. From Bayonne, it is only a 53 km ride with an elevation of 460 m.

Saint-Jean-Pied-de-Port is a Basque town in France and stands at the base of Ron Cevaux Pass. Pied-de-Port means the 'foot of the pass.'

The French routes of the Camino (Paris, Vezelay and Le Puy en Velay) all meet at Saint-Jean-Pied-de-Port and was traditionally the pilgrims' last refuge and a chance to rest before the arduous Pyrenees crossing. On our Camino de Santiago Cycle Challenge, Facebook page, one of our members who had completed the Camino from Saint-Jean, asked us why we had bypassed it. When I explained that I thought it was pushing it a little, he commented that it was probably the best decision we could have made.

There are plenty of places to stay in Saint-Jean, and lots of bars, shops and restaurants and they specialise in fromage de brebis, which is a local cheese. It is a gastronomic delight, try the local fresh trout and a pipérade omelette with peppers and Bayonne ham.

On Mondays there´s a market day with a difference as sheep and cattle are driven into the town. If you are in town at 5 pm, there is a communal game of bare-handed pelote, a game which is also a tradition in the Valencian region where I live.

Saint-Jean-Pied-de-Port to Tolosa
Hendaye to Tolosa

Now I will pick up the two routes that take us on to Tolosa.

One of the traditional routes is from Saint-Jean-Pied-de-Port to Pamplona. I have purposely omitted Pamplona for two reasons. Firstly, I have heard from many pilgrims that walking through Pamplona can be oppressively hot in June, July and August. It's a city with a long history of bull running and a traditional stop on the Camino, but it's just a city and many pilgrims bypass it for the simple reason they prefer to walk through forests, valleys and mountains than a big city.

I met one pilgrim called Sara and her route was taking her into Pamplona.

"It has to be done," she said.

"Why," I said, "why not head west into the national park, it's cooler?"

She looked at me blankly, "well, because it's part of the Camino."

As I write this chapter, I can't help reflecting on the conversation I'd had with Jan Vandersypen.

"Your Camino is personal," he said, "it's yours, walk where you want, be free, that's what The Way is all about."

The second reason I didn't want to take the route through Pamplona is that it's famous for bull-running. Pamplona is bullfighting country. In this modern age, torturing and then slaughtering such an elegant beast defies logic. In the second week of July they run them through the cobbled streets where many of the bulls lose their footing and break legs, some crash into walls and suffer fractured skulls and if that isn't bad enough they slaughter nearly 50 of them at the bull ring in the evenings.

When the poor bull is so weak that it can't even stand, the matador stabs it in the head with a dagger. I'm not sure what goes through the mind of the warped individual who does that. What possible pleasure can he derive from such an action? What level of satisfaction and pride can he take back home to his family in the evening? Will he tell them that he was so courageous that he killed a defenseless animal who didn't even have the strength to stand?

By all means, take in Pamplona on your Camino, but I'm boycotting it until they stop torturing bulls to death.

Saint-Jean-Pied-de-Port to Tolosa

As I mentioned, this route is not for the faint-hearted cyclist but takes in part of the beautiful and spectacular Basque National Park with glorious scenery from start to finish. The 97 km run with an elevation of 1,800 m is doable in one day, but you'll need an early start.

Top Tip: Hold back on the beer and wine the night before.

It really is wise to be on the road before 8 am and with a clear head. You need to be aiming for Elgorriaga before lunchtime because it's around eight to nine hours in the saddle.

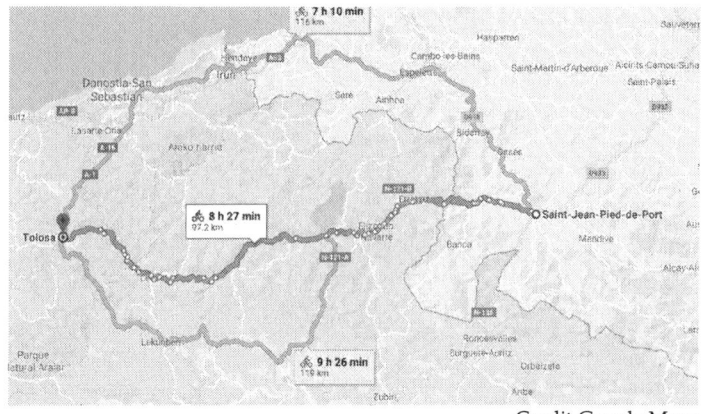

Credit Google Maps

The route follows the N121B minor road towards Erratzu, and from Legasa it switches to the NA170 in the direction of Leitza. After Leitza it's not a bad run into Tolosa, but by this point, you will be on the bottom of your reserves having completed two category one climbs.

Hendaye to Tolosa

I mentioned before that it's important to take rest days or easy days when attempting a challenge such as this. Allowing for some recovery time is essential, whether you are 20 years old or 65. Always remember that the professionals on the Tour de France have rest days. If it's good enough for them, it's good enough for us amateurs.

Credit Google Maps

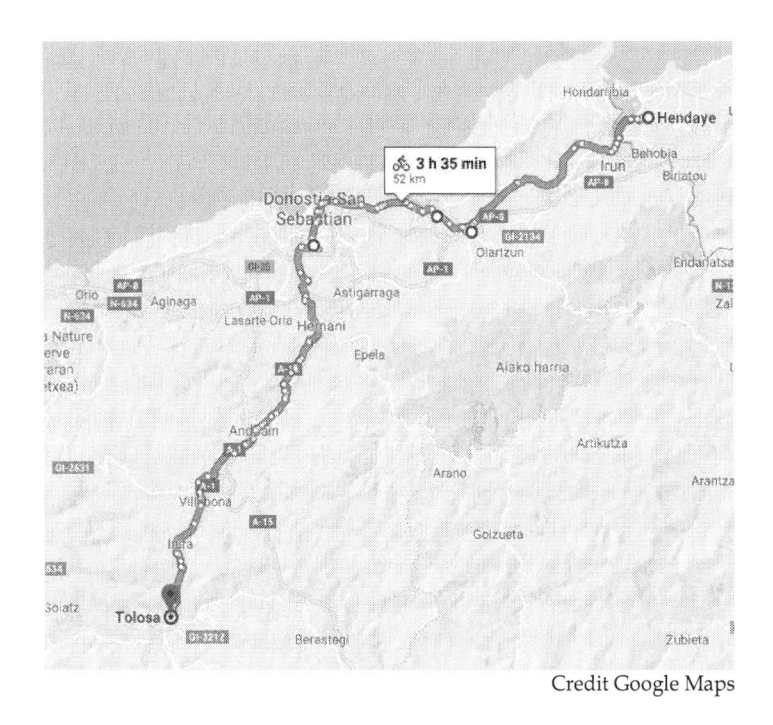

The run from Hendaye to Tolosa had a fair bit of elevation, but we classed it as an easy day because it was only a 55 km run. We would be hitting the Pyrenees for the first time.

We crossed the border into Spain at Irun, though saw no evidence of any border. It was industrial at first, on a few busy roads and wasn't particularly pleasant but we managed to put in about 17 km in the first hour before we then started to climb.

The GI 636 merged onto the GI 2638 and then returned to the GI 636.

We could now see the Pyrenees just ahead. We feared the worst, but to be honest, it wasn't that bad. By now, we had begun to toughen up and our muscles were somehow adapting to the stresses and strains placed on them. It was a weird feeling that, after two or three arduous days, we were beginning to feel quite good and we approached the three climbs of the day with a sort of 'bring it on' approach and once again, hills were our friends.

We passed Hernani and a signpost told us it was only 5 km to Villabona and only another eight or nine to Tolosa as the cycle path ran alongside the River Oria. We spotted a bar by a small village and rode across a bridge to see if it was open. It was hardly a village as there was the bar and nothing else. A blind dog stumbled from seat to seat bumping into the people's legs as they enjoyed their refreshing drinks and put the world to rights.

The trials and tribulations of the previous day had all but been forgotten. All of a sudden, the Camino Challenge was the greatest thing in the world. We were happy because we were enjoying a beer in the sunshine and we knew that our final destination was less than 15 km away. Google Maps told us it was mostly on the flat and the hard work of the day was behind us.

As we rolled into the town of Tolosa, we stopped again at the first bar we came across - it was becoming a bit of a habit. We had the obligatory Basque pintxos, small sandwiches, and by now, I could even spell it right. We washed them down with a few beers, a glass of wine or six for Caroline and by the time I started on my second beer, Dave had eventually decided what he wanted to drink.

We keyed in the directions for our accommodation for the evening and the GPS took us into the medieval part of town.

It was like stepping back in time. The medieval town is walled and the streets just narrow enough for a horse and cart, so it's pedestrian- and bicycle-friendly with bars, market shops and restaurants. The vibe was just right and it was the sort of place where you think to yourself, 'this is nice.'

The owner of the property arrived and let us in. We climbed two flights of stairs from a rather dingy passageway. I confess we weren't expecting very much. Again, this was only costing about 25€ a night each. How wrong we were. The door opened up into an elegant hallway which led straight to a huge bedroom that looked onto the old street from a wrought-iron balcony. On our Facebook group, you can see a photograph of Caroline on the balcony (19 June) with the caption Gannin oot the neet, which is Geordie for, "we are wandering out into town for the evening."

"This is mine", Caroline said, without even looking anywhere else.

The rest of the apartment didn´t disappoint. It was a vast rabbit warren of interconnecting rooms, bathrooms, a dining room and a huge lounge with oxblood leather chesterfield sofas. It was so good that I took a video and you can see this on the video that accompanies this book. The apartment was classy; everything about it was perfect and it reflected the ambience of the town.

It was so good we almost didn't want to go out and even considered finding a supermarket and eating in. The kitchen was well equipped, and I imagined the steaks sizzling in the large cast iron pan that hung from a hook on the wall.

But we decided we wanted to explore the town so we chilled for a couple of hours before heading out.

One of the downsides of only having a couple of weeks to cycle the Camino is not having the time to explore some of the really special places you come across. Tolosa was one of those places, and I urge anyone who comes into Spain from France to make a beeline for this beautiful town and spend at least a day there. By the time we ventured out, it was nearly eight o'clock and we were hungry.

Because we had to leave early the next morning, we didn't have time to see the old town hall built in the 17th century or the convent of Saint Francis on the Camino Real. Nor did we see the churches of Saint Clara, the Basque Gothic church of Saint Mary, Corpus Cristi or the 17th century Palace of Aranburu. In fact, there are more palaces than you could shake a stick at, like the 16th Century Palace of Atodo, the Palace of Justice and the Palace of Idiakez. Idiakez Palace was built in 1605 and stands on the walls of the town in the area of the old Puerta (gate) de Navarra.

I felt the history as we strolled through the old town looking for restaurants and when we left early the next morning, I promised myself I would return to Tolosa soon. As a side note, the Spanish footballer Xavi Alonso, formerly of Liverpool and now Real Madrid, is from Tolosa.

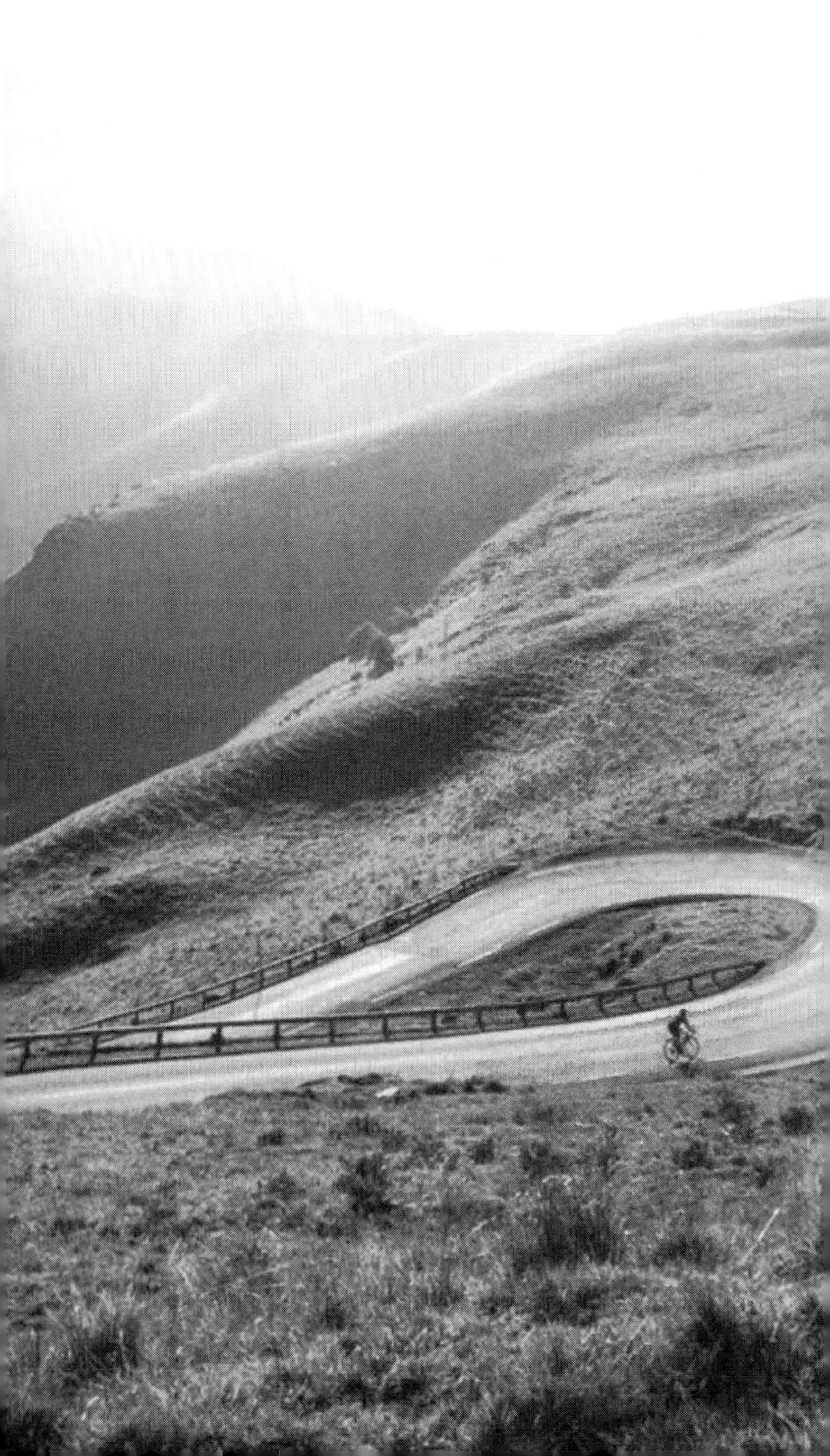

Day Six

Tolosa to Olazti / Olazagutía

The Pyrenees

Today we were hitting the first real mountains of the Pyrenees, heading due south out of Tolosa.
We were sad to leave the city and we rode in a soft drizzle, the first rain we had encountered on our trip since a few spots in Bordeaux.
We hadn't planned our accommodation for that evening, having decided to leave it to chance and we hoped to put in another 70 or 80 km, perhaps more, on our journey to Santiago.
As you can see on the map, there is a longer, tougher route via the GI 2635 but we decided against it. For seasoned club riders and younger folks it's worth considering as it's a spectacular ride.

It rained steadily for around 5 km as we cycled towards Alegría following the route of the main motorway, the A1. It was a steady but gentle climb before the going started to get a little tougher and as we passed a small village called Beasain, the gradient took a turn for the worst and the higher we climbed, the harder it rained.

At Zegama the road upped the pressure and we began cycling uphill along dozens of hairpin bends.

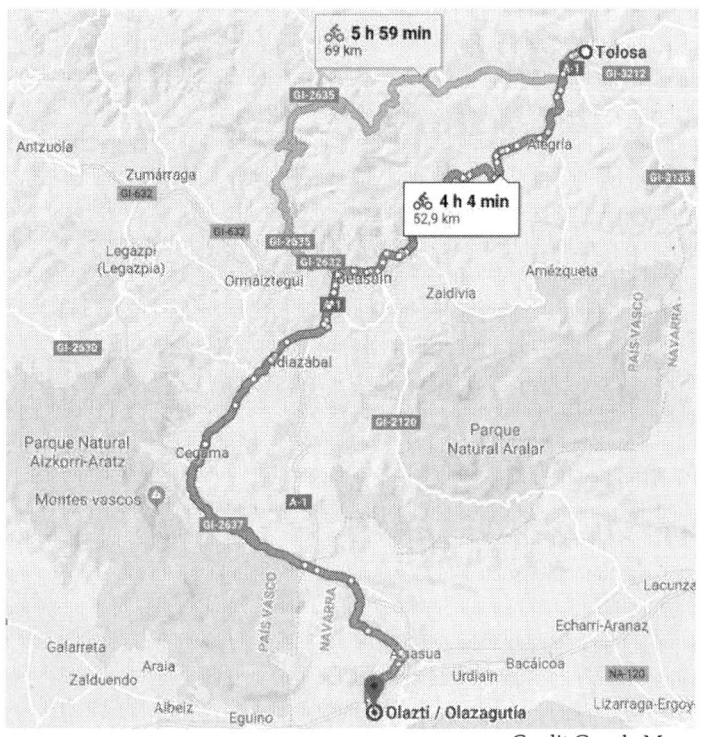

Credit Google Maps

We had been climbing about 6 km in the rain but our legs and our hearts coped well and as we discussed the climb on the way up, to a man (and Caroline) everybody said how much they were enjoying it. It made for a pleasant change to be cycling in cool temperatures instead of blistering heat.

We were now on the GI 2637 and passed a small hamlet called Zegama.

By the time we reached the top, it had been an 11 km climb and I was surprised to see that everyone was smiling and in good spirits. If you look at the Facebook group, you will see the live video (20 June). There is also a compilation video (3 July) of everything I have described in this book.

It had been a great morning, it was still only 1 pm and Map my Ride (Dave's app) told us we had cycled 35 km (I had forgotten to set the Relive app) and we were now looking forward to 15 km downhill and flat terrain in the direction of Vitoria Gasteiz.

We wondered how close we could get to Vitoria Gasteiz that day. It was another 67 km away and probably a step too far but if we could make it to Arrieta or even Argomaniz, we would be well ahead of schedule.

We were feeling confident and took an early lunch as we left the Basque Country for a short while and headed into the Navarra region that borders Rioja and Aragon.

It was early afternoon when the Google cycle route took us off the NA 1001 and onto a forest track. As we studied the route, we realised that the cycle route was heading towards Ziordia, effectively cutting around 5 km from the road journey.

Although it seemed like a good idea at the time, 3 or 4 km later, the murmurs of discontent started up again. We had been riding on tarmac roads most of the day and even though we climbed a lot that morning, it was pleasant going and relatively fast. Now we were in a forest encountering rocky terrain with tree roots sticking up all over the place. Once or twice we nearly came off and the route was like a long rollercoaster. It was up and down every view hundred metres and just when we thought we'd encountered the last of the hills, we turned a corner and there was another one ahead of us.

The rough ground was taking its toll on my backside as I still hadn't recovered from the day before and sensed that two big blisters were beginning to form on my arse.

Before the challenge, we had decided to fit hybrid tyres to our bikes because we knew that most of the route would be on tarmac roads or decent shale track and mountain bike tyres would hold us up.

It was undoubtedly the correct decision, but when we encountered anything like a mountain bike path, these tyres were absolutely useless because they had very little grip.

Dave, in particular, struggled to get a decent grip as his tyres were half an inch thinner than ours.

For the most part, the GPS cycle route worked well, but there was no way of knowing the exact type of track it was directing us to.

The track got rougher as we got deeper into the forest and after a couple of spills which could have been quite dangerous, we decided to head back to the road.

Our trip into the forest had cost us an additional eight to ten kilometres and more than an hour in time, but we were all relieved when we re-joined the N 1001 which ran into the N 1000 as we headed towards Alsasua (Altsasu).

We had no idea of the nightmare we were about to encounter as we trundled slowly into town.

The GPS screwed up, it was as simple as that and I can only think that the signal must have been intermittent. As we headed into town, it took us west, down a small street, past an albergue. Shortly after that, we started our two-hour, wild goose chase.

Even looking back on it now I can't begin to imagine what happened. We were in town, in an industrial estate looking for a track that ran alongside the River Arakil which would take us towards our next destination of Olazti / Olazagutía and from there we would head in the direction of Vitoria Gasteiz.

It seemed so easy and the town isn't even that big; it's not as if we were in the middle of Madrid!

After two hours of going around in circles, we made for the albergue. My backside was in ribbons, Caroline was complaining, and we decided to stay at the albergue for the evening even though we were well short of our intended target. The wild goose chase and the debacle in the forest had finished us.

The albergue was closed and there was no sign of anybody around and then a strange thing happened. A man showed up in a white minibus and I wandered over to him thinking he might have something to do with the albergue. He didn't.

"When does it open?" I asked.

He shrugged his shoulders.

I explained what had happened and he smiled and said that 'everyone gets lost here.' He had seen walkers in tears because they can't make it out of town.

"Really?"

"Yes," he nodded.

He asked where we were going.

"Olatzi," I replied.

He jumped in his van, "follow me."

The rest of the gang were mystified as they had just been sitting by the side of the road while I spoke to him. I explained that our guardian angel was taking us to where we needed to be and while he tootled along at 12 km an hour, we dutifully followed behind.

He took us out of the industrial area, over about four roundabouts and into town. There were no road signs and certainly no clues to where Olatzi was.

We took a fairly straight route through town passing at least a dozen side streets on both sides and then crossed over a big flyover with a motorway running underneath. At a big roundabout, we swung left and there were still no signs for road numbers or Olatzi / Olazagutia. I was cursing to myself; no wonder people get lost.

We joined the main road, the A1, for about 1 km and then branched off and only then did we see the sign for Olatzi / Olazagutia.

As we pulled up into the town, we couldn't thank our friend enough. Caroline tried to shove a 10€ note into his hand, but he wouldn't take it. He said he had walked the Camino many times and he was only too happy to help.

He had conveniently pulled up outside a hotel which appeared to be closed, but he asked us if we wanted to stay the night.

"Yes!" we all cried out in unison.

Well, that's not strictly true, because Caroline pointed out that we were at least 20 km short of our intended destination. I take my hat off to her, she did indeed want to put in another 20 clicks, but it wasn't going to happen and she was outvoted by four to one - Dave, Gary, me and my arse.

We were wrecked. The Map my Ride data read just short of 70 km and it was enough for one day.

Minibus Man told us to go into the butcher shop next to the hotel as they were the owners. The hotel was closed, but he was certain they would open it up for us.

He was right. They asked how many rooms we wanted and told us that the hotel was closed but if we could give them an hour to prepare some beds and linen we were in business.

We found a bar along the street and once again we laughed about what had happened. We reassured ourselves that it had been a good day for the most part, but our 70 km cycle had somehow cost us 17 km. When I logged the route into Google Maps and put in our starting destination to where we had ended up it said it was 53 km ride.

We couldn't go on like this. We needed to take drastic action.

Later that evening, while we enjoyed dinner in one of the local bars, I called my mate Steve Nash again and explained our predicament. I told him about getting lost and the disaster in the forest. Steve had been on the Camino several times and explained that GPS was good at times but couldn't be relied upon. My main concern was that it could direct us onto unsuitable cycle paths.

We discussed our options and decided that from then on we would try and complete the Camino by cycling on roads wherever possible. Gary said that it might put a few kilometres onto our route, but at the end of the day, it was always faster. We all agreed.

It was time to do a rethink and to analyse the Spanish roads and apply the Google map filters to keep us off the main roads.

Top Tip. I also received some good advice for my blistered bum. Nivea Cream - the stuff in the navy-blue tin. Rub as much of it as you can into the seat of your cycling shorts and repeat the exercise two or three times a day.

As we tucked into our main course that evening, Dave said that tomorrow we would have to put in a 100 km day to get us back on schedule.

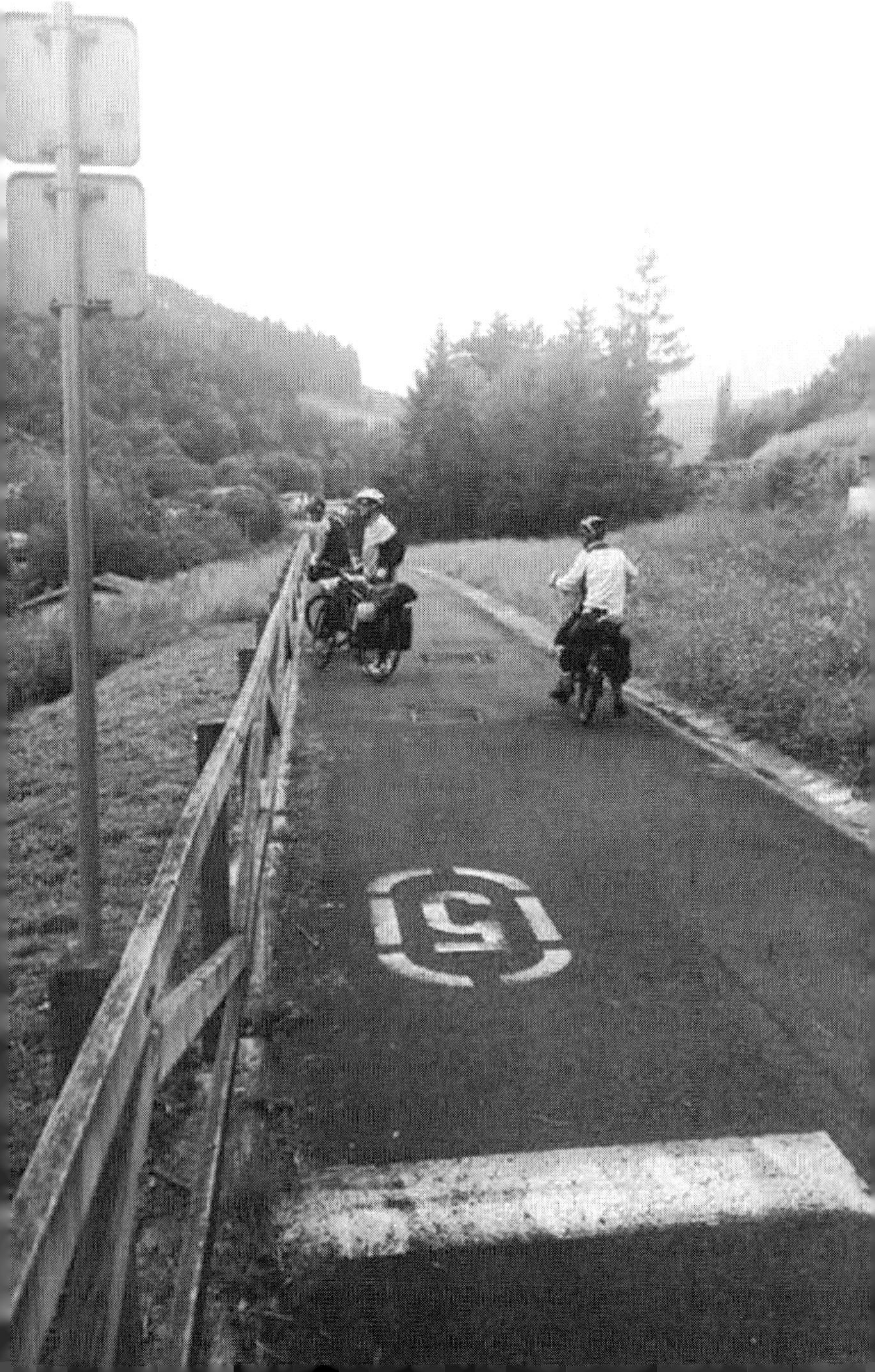

Day Seven

Olazti to Ameyugo

73 kilometres before lunch

For once we had an early night. The thought of a 100 km day curtailed our drinking and in any case, the bar had closed early. The kitchen closed at 8.30 pm and the barman was keen to go home soon after 10.00 pm. It was probably a good thing.
We decided to get away early and left well before 8.00 am; the plan was to get a little breakfast any time after 10 km.
It worked well, and we set off on the A313B, a quiet and narrow single carriageway road. There was also a well-signed cycle path that ran along at least half of this road. It's well worth keeping an eye out for these tracks as there were miles of them in this part of the country. They are concrete,

not rough road and always run next to the main road.

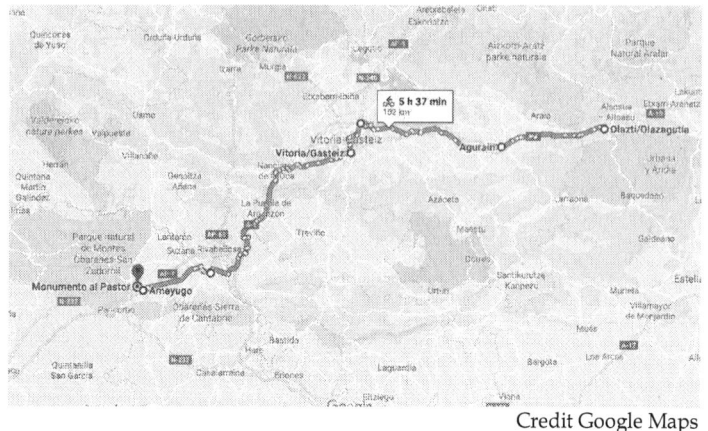

Credit Google Maps

After 12 km we came across a small industrial estate and spotted a sign for a café where we had breakfast. There was also a shop and after we'd eaten, we stocked up on chocolate, dried fruit and nuts, cereal bars and drinks.

From Agurain we took another single carriageway road, the A3100 and then the A4109. For almost 10 km it was either all downhill or on the flat until we reached a village called Arrieta Alava and after 10 km, we started to climb to Argomaniz. After that, it was all downhill to Vitoria Gasteiz, our first big town of the day. It wasn't even 11.00 am and we had clocked up nearly 47 km. We were flying!

It's incredible how a few hours of pleasant cycling can make you forget about yesterday's bad experiences and suddenly cycling can be the greatest sport in the world again.

We were in no doubt that we would hit our 100 km target for the day, and we had tents, so even if we had to sleep by the side of the road, we would find somewhere close to a bar or restaurant where we could eat and pitch the tents nearby. As I said in previous chapters, lightweight tents and sleeping bags are an excellent insurance policy.

The GPS took us through and out of Vitoria and we clocked up another easy 30 km along the A3302, A 2662 and the N1 to Arminon where we had lunch.

We were ecstatic when we checked Map my Ride and it registered 73 km, without getting lost once!

We thanked the gods and of course, Steve Nash, who had persuaded me to stick to the minor roads and plan the route ourselves instead of trying to keep to the GPS cycle routes. It had been a good decision.

We ordered beers and some pintxos at a roadside bar and then just for the hell of it we ordered some more. After all, we had less than 30 km to go before hitting our target for the day.

We were in that little bar on the border of the Basque Country and Castile and León for nearly two hours and we congratulated ourselves on how clever we all were. We were stuffed when we left and as we cycled slowly out of the village, we looked up ahead and saw a huge hill.

That wasn't in the bloody script! We climbed for a kilometre. It was crazy and painful and we had to make several stops before we reached Rivabellosa, but then thankfully we were back onto flat roads on the N1.

Top Tip: Do not cycle on a full stomach, eat little and often despite the temptations.

At Miranda de Ebro we continued on the N1 past Orón, where the single carriageway got quieter and we were back into a National Park. We were now only 10 km short of the 100 km mark and we were determined to press on and make it.

The milestone, (or should that be the kilometre stone?) came in the shape of a tiny village called Ameyugo, just off the N1 and as we turned into the small hamlet, we spotted a bar on the right-hand side.

We had made it, just over 100 km in one day.

In the bar, we asked about accommodation. There was nothing in the village, but the girl said there was a lovely campsite at the Monument to the Shepherd (Monumento al Pastor,) less than 2 km away.

It was happy days all round. We had a couple of drinks and then cycled to the campsite. We turned off the N1 after about a kilometre and then cycled a very steep gradient for 800 m before spotting the reception area to the campsite. They had space available and a restaurant on site. As we booked our pitches for the night, Caroline asked if there was a hotel nearby. The owner said yes, 5 or 6 km away. Caroline's face fell, but the owner announced that if Caroline wanted a lift there, she would be happy to take her, check her in and then bring her back to the campsite restaurant for the night.

And that's precisely what happened.

I highly recommend the campsite of the Monument to the Shepherd; it is high on a hill with spectacular vistas and the food is excellent and very reasonably priced.

They don't appear to have a website, but Google 'Camping Monumento del Pastor' and you´ll find them easily. Booking ahead is not necessary.

As if the day couldn't get any better, we found out via Facebook friends that two donors had pledged another 1,600€ to the Marie Curie charity. We had 1,000€ from Gary Burr who heads the Giving4Giving Charity and 600€ from the owners of The Shamrock Bar in Benidorm and Brew Rock in Albir.

Caroline didn't even have to take a taxi back to her hotel as we were last out of the bar and surprise, surprise, the owner gave her a lift.

Dave, Gary and I wandered back to our tents just before midnight and we slept like babies.

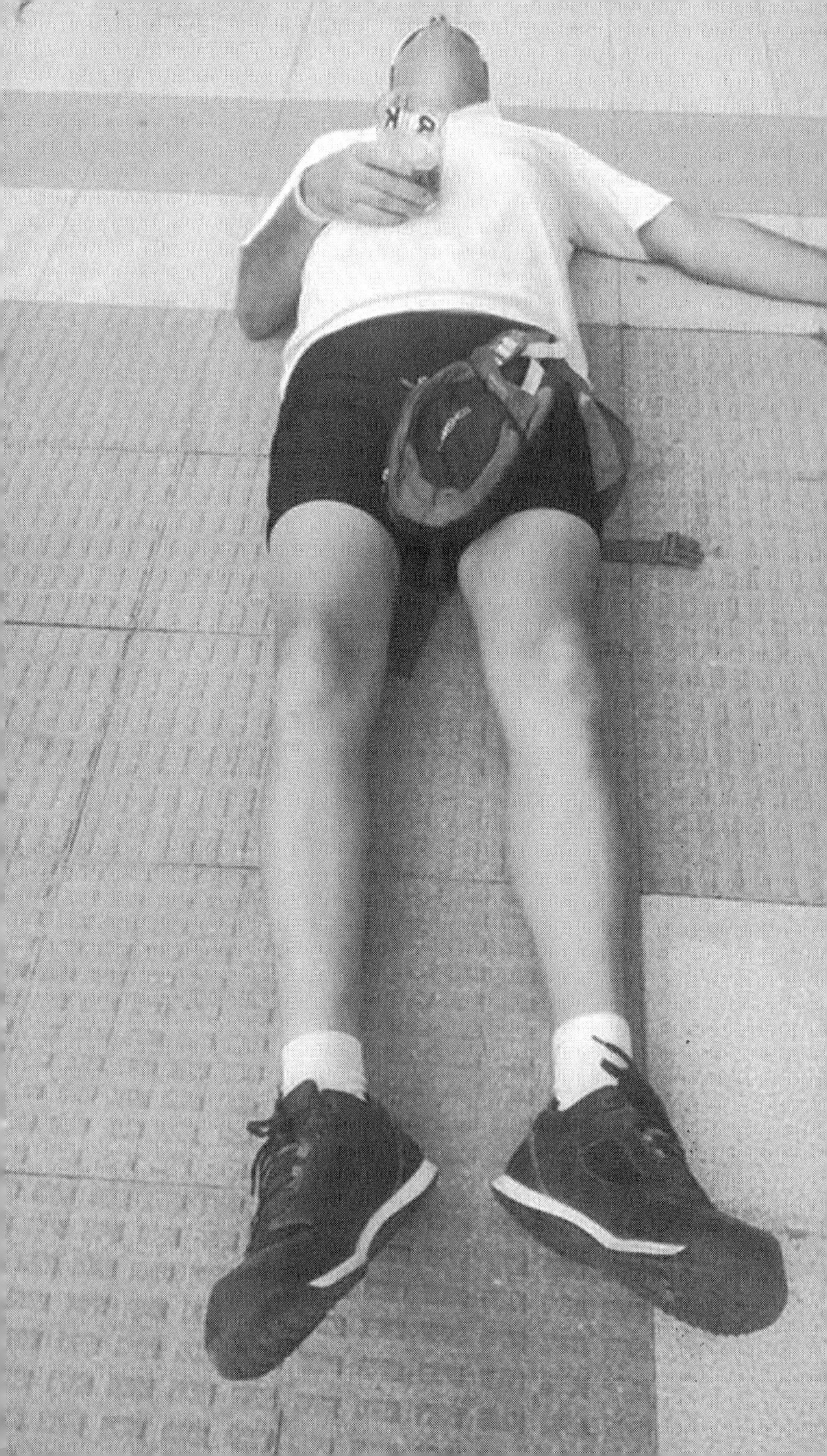

Day Eight

Ameyugo to La Nuez de Arriba

A big mistake

It was a late start by the time we got going, which wasn't ideal. The boys and I had been up before 7.00 am, as always happens when you are camping, but Caroline only arrived after 9.00 am. She´d had to rely on a lift from the owner who didn't believe in opening too early. While we put Caroline's kit back on her bike, we sensed that the owner wasn't going to be very quick getting the café open so decided to head off and look for somewhere to eat en route.

We filled our water bottles up at the toilets inside the cafe.

"Let's put in ten km," Dave said, "and get some breakfast after that."

It sounded like a good idea at the time.

When we cycled off down the hill into the sunshine, we were feeling good. We had completed 519km, which was just over half of our 1,000-kilometre challenge, at an average of 74km per day. For the first time since we had left Bordeaux Airport we knew that completing the challenge was now a real possibility and it would have to take something disastrous to stop us.

We saw no reason to change the road option as it worked well yesterday, nor did we book any campsites or apartments. We were all keen to see how far we could get.

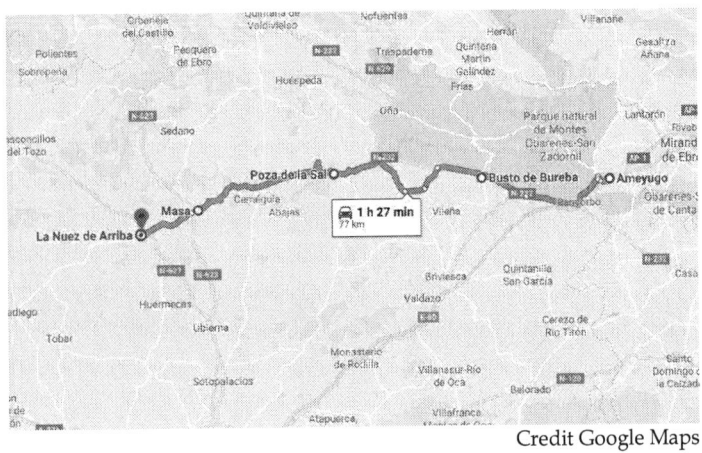

Credit Google Maps

We followed the N1 for about 12 km but unfortunately didn't see any open cafes or shops on the way which was a little disappointing. It was a quiet road, but the first kilometres were quite tough; not an overly steep gradient but steady uphill most of the way. The N1 eventually led onto the N232 and by now we were 20 km in without any breakfast. We had a few pieces of chocolate and a packet of salted nuts between us but eventually everything disappeared.

We had been stupid. There had been a small shop at the campsite and not one of us had the foresight to fill our panniers. We had been basking in the glory of a 100 km ride and hadn't even thought about the next day.

We turned onto a minor road and rode into the village of Busto de Bureba, figuring there would be a café or shop.

No luck, it was a ghost town of four or five small streets with most of the houses boarded up. This was something we saw a lot of during our journey. Many of these rural villages are dying, with the youngsters moving to the bigger towns and cities for work.

Top Tip. Don't plan your route via villages that you assume will have somewhere to eat and drink.

At least there was a drinking fountain and we took the opportunity to fill up our water bottles.

We went back onto the N232 and cycled for another 10 km. We were still out of luck, and there was nothing along the road but as we turned off onto the CL 633, we passed a barely noticeable village slightly up a hill. A woman was working a small allotment and I asked her if there is a bar in the village. She nodded and smiled.

"Is it open?"

"Si."

We were in business.

The village is called Cornudilla. It has a small town square and a big church (there is always a big church,) and although there were several boarded-up houses, sure enough, directly in front of us was a bar and it was open.

A bar with no bloody food!

Well, that isn´t strictly true, it had crisps and ice creams, but no tapas, no menu of the day and no pintxos or bocadillos.

I couldn't quite believe it, but we didn't let it get us down because the next town, which looked a decent size, was only 7 km away.

So, we had a couple of drinks and some crisps and set off up the hill to Poza de la Sal of which the literal translation means 'the pool of salt'.

It was a 7 km climb up to Poza and it was hot. The gradient was steady with just a couple of steep inclines, but we managed it no problem. It was here that we made two of our biggest mistakes of the Camino.

Now, you may be reading this book and thinking, 'these guys made a lot of mistakes.' Well, you wouldn't be far from the truth. It was our first ever long-distance cycle and boy did we get a lot of it wrong.

If you remember from my introduction, I'd searched high and low for a cycling book that would help me prepare and plan, but the reality is that there isn't such a book and that's why I´m writing this one. And, because this is the first edition, I am going to document where we went wrong, so that you, my fellow cyclist - won't!

This book isn't like John Brierley's books and you won't find perfection within these pages, nor the ideal way to cycle the Camino. Remember Brierley is on the 19th edition and has around 30 Caminos under his belt. Just imagine how many mistakes he made on the earlier trips.

Who knows, in ten years´ time you may be reading the perfect way to cycle the Camino by Ken Scott, but then again perhaps not. We suffered at times and it wasn't fun. But it was a laugh a minute, or at least it was when we eventually made it to the bar in the evenings.

Anyway, back to Poza de la Sal. The town is located on the side of a mountain at a height of 750 m and is fortified and protected by Castillo de los Rojas, the Red Castle.

Poza de la Sal is so named because of its salt flats which have been in production since Roman times.

The geological formation of Poza's incredible salt pool in the Cantabrian Mountains is the largest in Europe with a radius of 2.5 km.

In the late 1800s, the town had a population of 3,255 inhabitants, most of whom were directly involved in salt production. As I mentioned early in the chapter, these small Spanish towns have gradually declined over the years and now the population of Poza is less than 400.

It's well worth a visit as it has plenty of shops and a pretty town square.

When we arrived in the town we pulled up next to a dry drinking fountain. No sooner had we voiced our disappointment when a little old fellow appeared from behind a gate.

"Tengo agua," he said, (I have water) and beckoned us through his gate.

His name was Tomas and he had a natural well where we filled up our bottles. He had a large allotment with every type of vegetable you can think of and he had cockerels and hens too. He was spraying his garden with a sprinkler and we stood underneath and had a refreshing shower while Tomas looked on and laughed.

He hadn´t finished, and he pulled open a fridge that was tucked under an outside kitchen and handed us four ice cold beers. How could we say no?

We spent an hour with Tomas and as the beers filled our stomachs, we forgot how hungry we all were. It was now lunchtime and we hadn't eaten anything substantial since the night before.

Our next point on the map was a place called Masa and as we discussed the route, Tomas explained that we had climbed the hard road and it was all downhill and flat to Masa.

"Facil," he said.

"What does that mean?" Gary asked.

"Easy," I said.

I asked him if there was a bar or a restaurant and he nodded with a grin. Masa was signposted 20 km out at Poza de la Sal, which is always a good sign as it means that the town is relatively large.

The small hamlets are usually not signposted until just a few kilometres out.

As we said goodbye to Tomas, we tried to give him some money for the beers, but he flatly refused. I stood proud with my chest puffed out. This is the country I now call home and I told my Geordie mates that this was typical of Spain.

Now, at this point in proceedings we made two monumental errors and looking back now I can't think for the life of me how we hadn't learned from previous days' mistakes or heeded the advice handed down by Steve Nash.

Mistake number one was that we didn't eat. It was lunchtime and there were bars and restaurants by the score, so what were we thinking? The conversation went something like this.

"Shall we eat?"

"Nah.."

"Why not?"

"It's 20 km downhill, that's less than an hour away, let's eat there."

"Okay."

I would like to point a finger of blame at someone, but the truth is that it was a unanimous decision.

Mistake number two bordered on the worst decision ever made in modern history, worse than Hitler's assault on Russia in the winter, worse than Cameron's gamble on Brexit, worse than rejecting the unknown author, JK Rowling and her first Harry Potter book.

We were totally out of provisions, no chocolate, cheese, bread, muesli bars, nothing. Our cupboards were bare and in an act of sheer stupidity, we cycled past the town of Poza de la Sal and its supermarkets and shops, convinced that Masa was just a short ride away.

We climbed out of the village, turned through a few S-bends and climbed again. We climbed the first 2 km, which gave us stunning views of Poza and we stopped by the side of the road.

Dave dared to suggest that Tomas had got it wrong.

"Don't worry," I said, "it will level out soon and it will be a sweet 18 km downhill."

It was at least another 8 km climb to the top of the mountain which was ridiculously steep at times and we were on the bottom of our energy reserves by the time we reached the top.

"Surely all downhill to Masa?" Caroline asked.

I said nothing. I was concerned because as far as the eye could see, the landscape was flat. What was worse is that there was a strong head wind blowing straight into our faces.

We struggled on. About 5 km from Masa, Dave ran out of water and by the time we reached Masa, everybody was out of water. Not one of us had a spare bottle in our panniers. I think those last 10 km cycling through the wind farm on the enormous plateau of the Calabrian Mountains was the worst bit, at times it felt as if we weren't moving an inch.

By the time we got to Masa, I wanted to cycle back and take it out on Tomas. It had been three hours since we'd left Poza.

As soon as we pulled into Masa, I spotted a drinking fountain on the right-hand side of the road and we pulled over and drank like fish.

We sat on an old park bench under a tree and laughed like hell. We had screwed up again. It was almost as if every other day, a disaster found us.

It was now nearly 5.00 pm. We were all lightheaded and running on empty and as I casually glanced at the layout of the town, a horrible thought crossed my mind. It looked like another bloody ghost town with no sign of any life, no bars, no restaurants, no shops, not even a garage. It was the sort of town that had a few buildings and houses on both sides of the road and not much else.

I feared the worst.

As awful thoughts crossed my mind, a door to a house opened and a family casually strolled out of the front door. I wandered over and asked if there was a bar in the village.

"No."

"A shop?"

"No."

There was nothing. We couldn't believe it and when I asked where the next bar or shop was the old grandad pointed over my shoulder in the direction we had just come, "Poza de la Sal," he said.

I smiled and pointed in the other direction, "we are heading that way."

He nodded, laughed and said, "30 km."

I swear my knees nearly buckled. Surely he was mistaken.

"No, the next shop is at Aguilar."

I explained that our group hadn't eaten since the previous evening, I told them that we had cycled 75 km from Ameyugo without a scrap of food. They seemed impressed and shocked at the same time. I asked if they had any food in the house that we could buy, some cheese and bread, perhaps a little ham.

They shook their heads.

Bastards!

Of course, they had food.

They closed and locked the door, walked to their car and drove off.

I relayed the bad news to everyone as we sat under the shade of the tree for the next 40 minutes planning what to do. Not one of us had the energy even to argue, we were strangely calm and debated whether we had the reserves to cycle another 30 km without food. We drank more water. There was nothing for it; we had to soldier on until we found somewhere. If the worst came to the worst, we had our tents and sleeping bags and we could sleep somewhere. We would get some rest and get up early the following day before the sun got too hot.

"Even if we can get 10 km in," Gary said, "that's only 20 to do tomorrow."

We weren't going to die; we knew that because we had plenty of water. We could go without food for a day, no problem. It wasn't what we wanted to do and it wouldn't be a fun night, but we would make it. I was quite surprised at the positive attitude of the group.

We took on lots of water and made sure our bottles were full and climbed on our bikes as we cycled at a snail's pace out of the village.

After 6 km we came to the crossroads of the N627 and we spotted a small blue hotel sign, the one with a bed on and underneath it read 2 km.

We looked at Google Maps; it was a place called La Nuez de Arriba.

"Probably another ghost town," Caroline said, "the hotel probably closed years ago."

I looked the village up on Wikipedia. Population 27.

It didn't sound right; how can a village with a population of 27 have a hotel? Nevertheless, we cycled into the village. I think it's fair to say that after the day we'd had, none of us held out much hope.

There was a small hotel in La Nuez de Arriba and it was open. The smiles were back on our faces; we couldn't believe our luck. Before the young girl even checked us in, we explained where we had cycled from and the fact we hadn't eaten all day and begged her to make us some sandwiches. My faith in humanity was instantly restored as she returned ten minutes later with a plate of sandwiches and four tins of cold beer. It hardly touched the sides. We had hit the jackpot as she told us that we could have an evening meal a little later on. She was making a speciality soup and the main course was chicken and vegetables. Halleluiah!

A casa rural is a small country hotel or apartment, similar to a gite in France and this was the first time we had stayed in one. For 35€ per person, we had dinner, bed and breakfast.

It was first-class and if you are anywhere near La Nuez de Arriba on your travels, make sure this casa rural is on your list of places to stay and tell Maria she saved four cyclists' lives!

It is also listed on Airbnb, or you can call them direct on (+34) 652 573 226, Maria speaks decent English.

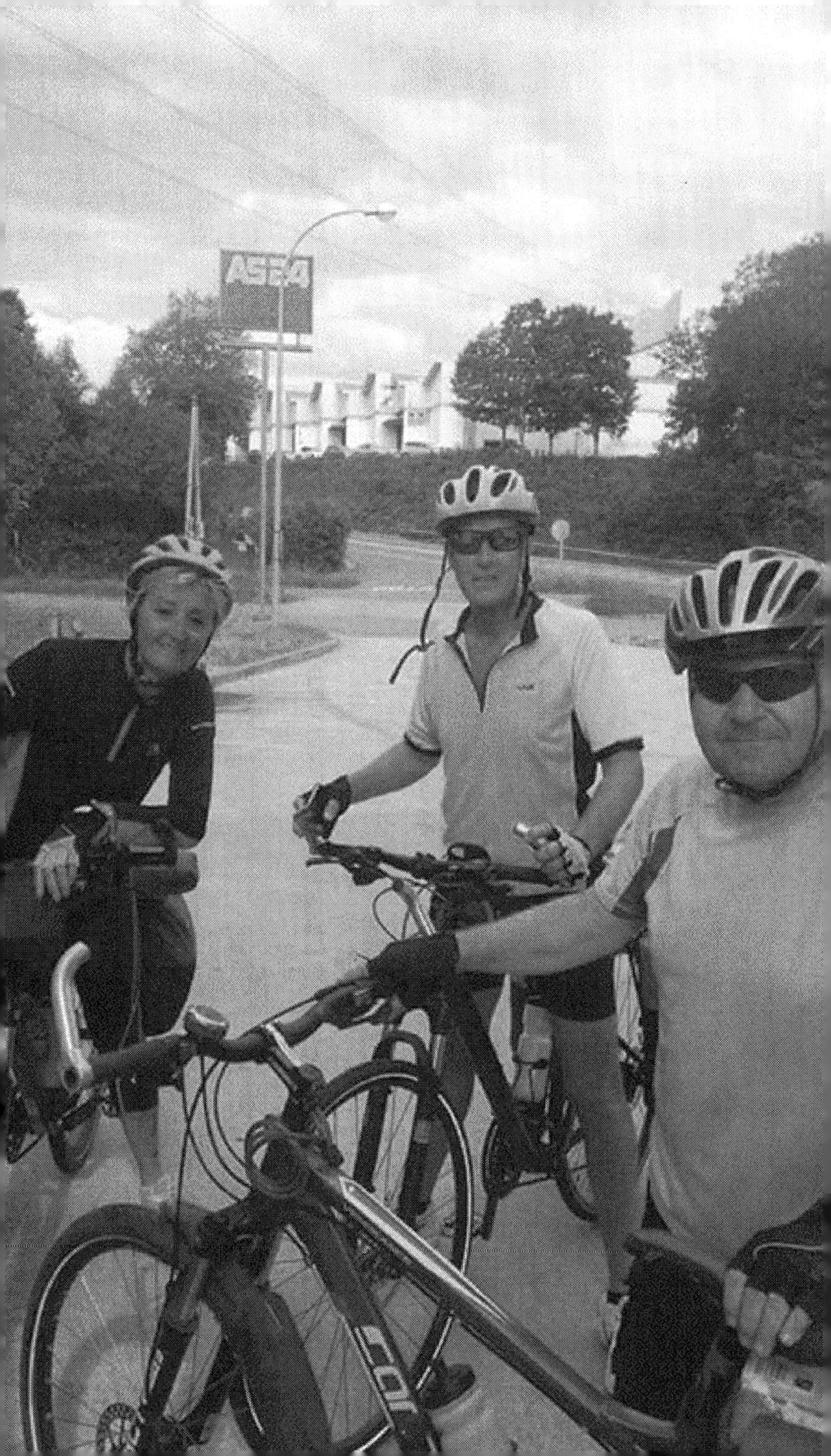

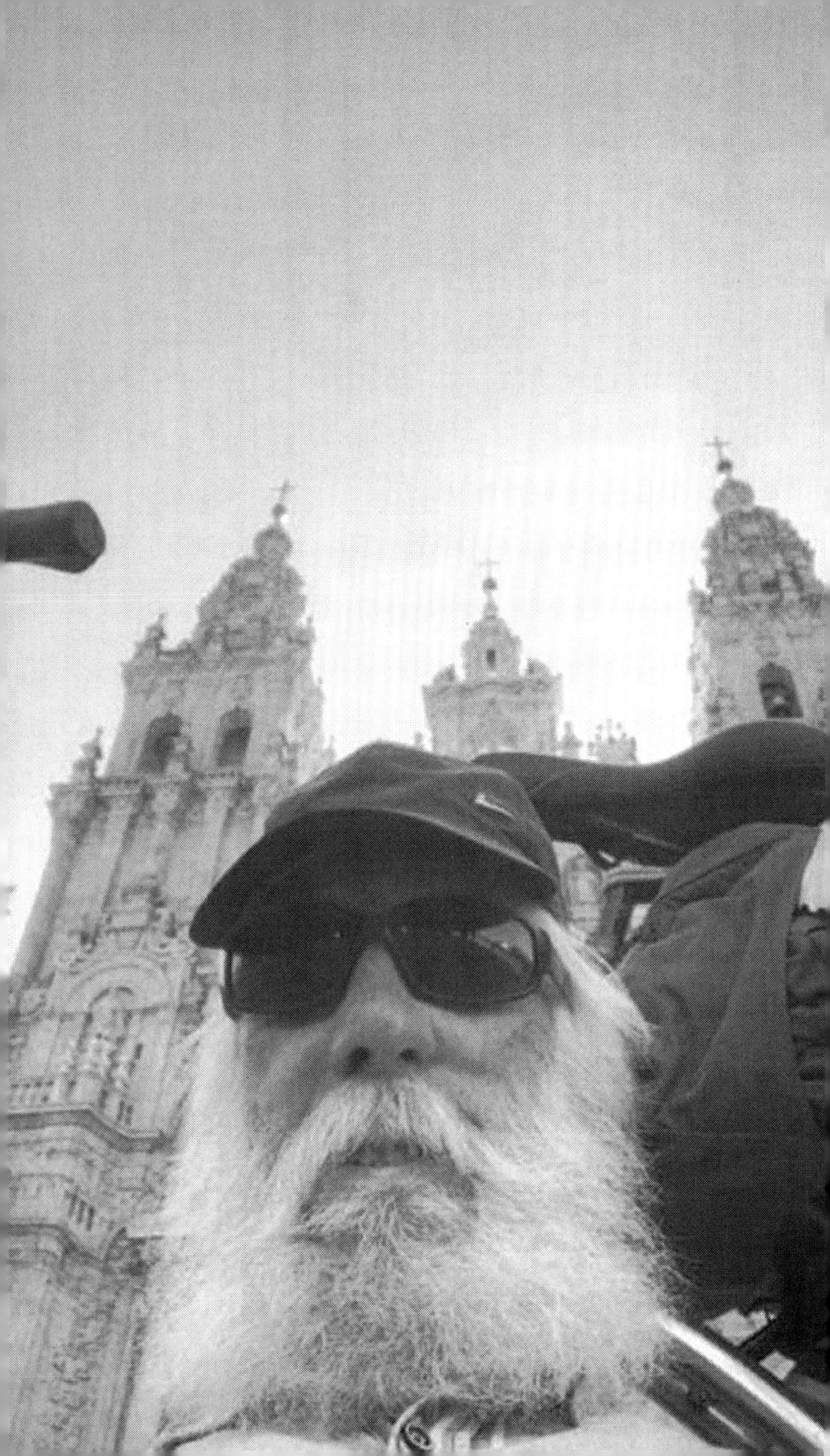

Day Nine

Nuez de la Arriba to Carrion de los Condes

Donald Sutherland

Cycling hundreds of kilometres on the Camino is the perfect way to clear your head and it also tells you a about the kind of person you are. As we cycled out of Nuez and picked up the CL 633, it immediately took us onto a reasonably steep climb again, the last thing we wanted after Maria's fine breakfast.

But rather than start moaning or thinking how unfair life was sometimes, it was a case of 'bring it on you bastards.'

If we couldn't be broken yesterday, there was no way it was going to happen today. Our panniers were also full of sandwiches and fruit that Maria had given us. There was no way were we going to get caught out again and of course, we'd had a decent breakfast. We felt great as we cycled out of the village.

My body was also coping well. This was our 9th day and I felt very strong and very fit. We climbed for 5 km and afterwards, a fast road took us downhill for more than 10 km to a town called Villamayor de Treviño and then onto Melgar de Fermantel.

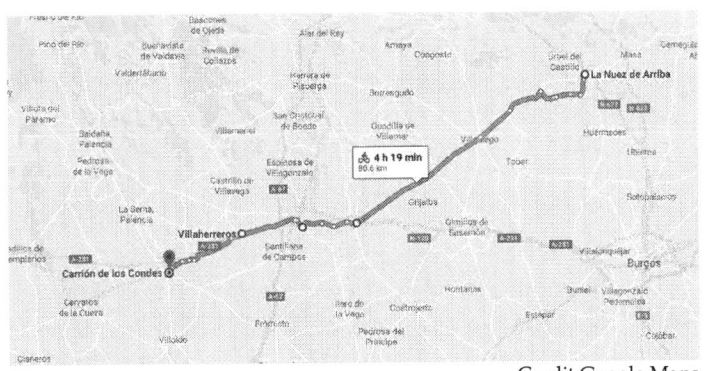

Credit Google Maps

The roads were superb single carriageways that snaked through the countryside of Castile and León. As we passed signs on the road which read Castile y León, I noticed that occasionally either one of the two word (Castile, León) had been blacked out or crossed out. This is all to do with independence and the fierce desire of a lot of Spaniards to avoid change at all costs and retain their cultural identity so they can wave their own flags.

Once upon a time The Kingdom of León and the Kingdom of Castile kept different parliaments, had different coins and different laws, right up until the Modern Era when Spain, like other European states, centralized governmental powers. I'm sure it all made economic sense and so instead of separate states, the autonomous community of Castile and León was born. But clearly, not everyone agrees. It's the same in the area of Valencia where I live, most of the road signs are in Spanish and Valenciano, which to me is a waste of space, a waste of steel and waste of paint. Never mind the carbon footprint, as long as we can have a sign that we can read twice then that's okay. Even though where I live is a huge tourist area, some locals see fit to black-out the Spanish words to remind everyone how fiercely Valencian the region is and that they don´t really consider themselves to be Spanish.

We rolled into Melgar de Fermantel to get a drink and some cash from an ATM. There appeared to be some sort of fiesta about to start; it was busy and everyone was dressed up. The bar we sat in brought free plates of tapas and we tucked in as they encouraged us to eat more. What a difference from yesterday, now people were throwing food at us.

We would have loved to hang around but earlier on we had decided to try and squeeze in another 100 km day so after stuffing our faces we set off.

The 100 km day didn't happen, Caroline was complaining of being saddle sore and after 85 km we approached the town of Carrion de los Condes on the A 231 on the Autovia Camino Santiago. It looked a decent sized place with plenty of shops and signs for a few hotels. There were lots of bars with people sitting outside in the sunshine and it had a friendly vibe to it. I mentioned Steve's advice to eat and sleep where you could and for once no one argued.

As we entered the town, there was a sign for a campsite and we decided to take a look. Caroline was set on a hotel for the evening so as the lads set off for the campsite, she made a few phone calls and tried the Airbnb app. After about ten minutes trying with no luck, Dave called. He said the campsite was fabulous with a big bar and restaurant on site. Caroline shrugged her shoulders, "okay, let's go for it, what the hell."

It was a lovely spot by the river and by the time we arrived, Dave and Gary's tents were already pitched. They gave us a hand and then we took a shower and headed for the bar.

Strange things happen on the Camino. At times it's as if you in another dimension, as if you're in a different body and a different mindset altogether. We were all totally chilled and at peace with the world - and for once with each other! It was as if someone had flicked a big switch and put us into laidback mode. As we came out the shower nobody spoke too much and even Caroline seemed content with her little pitch for the night.

Now, on any other holiday I've ever been on, after a shower and a change of clothes it was exploration time, especially if we knew there were bars or restaurants to visit. And yet, as we enjoyed that first drink in the campsite bar in Carrion de los Condes, the same thing happened that happened the night before in the hotel at Nuez de la Arriba. No one wanted to go anywhere. I think it must be a fatigue thing, a 'listen to your body' moment. Our bodies didn't want to walk or cycle another step. It was no more than two hundred metres to the centre of town, but in the discussion that ensued during that first round, we all agreed to stay put.

We were content and why not? We had cycled well over halfway to our goal. The beer was cold and we could smell the food aromas drifting through from the kitchen. Our beds for the night were only 25 m away so what was the point of walking into town?

And if it couldn't get any better, Donald Sutherland walked into the bar. Think Donald Sutherland in The Hunger Games but ten years older.

It was Dave who spotted him and Dave being Dave couldn't help himself. He was so subtle.

"Hey, Donald."

'Donald' wandered over and said hello. I had to look twice; my God this man was the double of Sutherland, one of the finest actors to grace this planet. It transpired that Jan Vandersypen, a Belgian, has been mistaken for Donald Sutherland about 'a thousand times', and did this man have some stories. He told us of a time when on a bus in Paris, a policeman boarded to check some ID and as soon as he saw Jan, insisted on having his photograph taken with him. Despite Jan trying to explain he wasn't the Canadian actor, the policeman didn't believe him and thought 'Donald' was trying to remain incognito.

Jan told me a story about a possible connection with the real Donald Sutherland, something that the actor knows nothing about. I don't think it's right to tell the story in this book, but I have written to Donald and if I ever get a reply and he allows the story to come out I will post it to my website, www.kenscottbooks.com

Suffice to say, Jan's high forehead, the eyes and the nose bear an uncanny resemblance to the actor.

Jan was cycling the Camino too, on an electric bike. He is over 70 years of age and electric bikes are not cheating for anyone of that age. He was cycling 2,200 km from Belgium; he has been walking the Camino for over 20 years and started biking it a few years back so that he could cover more ground.

Jan is an interesting guy and I warmed to him straight away. He said some things that had a profound effect on me. He left way too early that night, but I sensed our paths were destined to cross again; it was meant to be.

More on Jan in later chapters. If anyone needs to write a book on the Camino, it's this man.

SANTIAGO

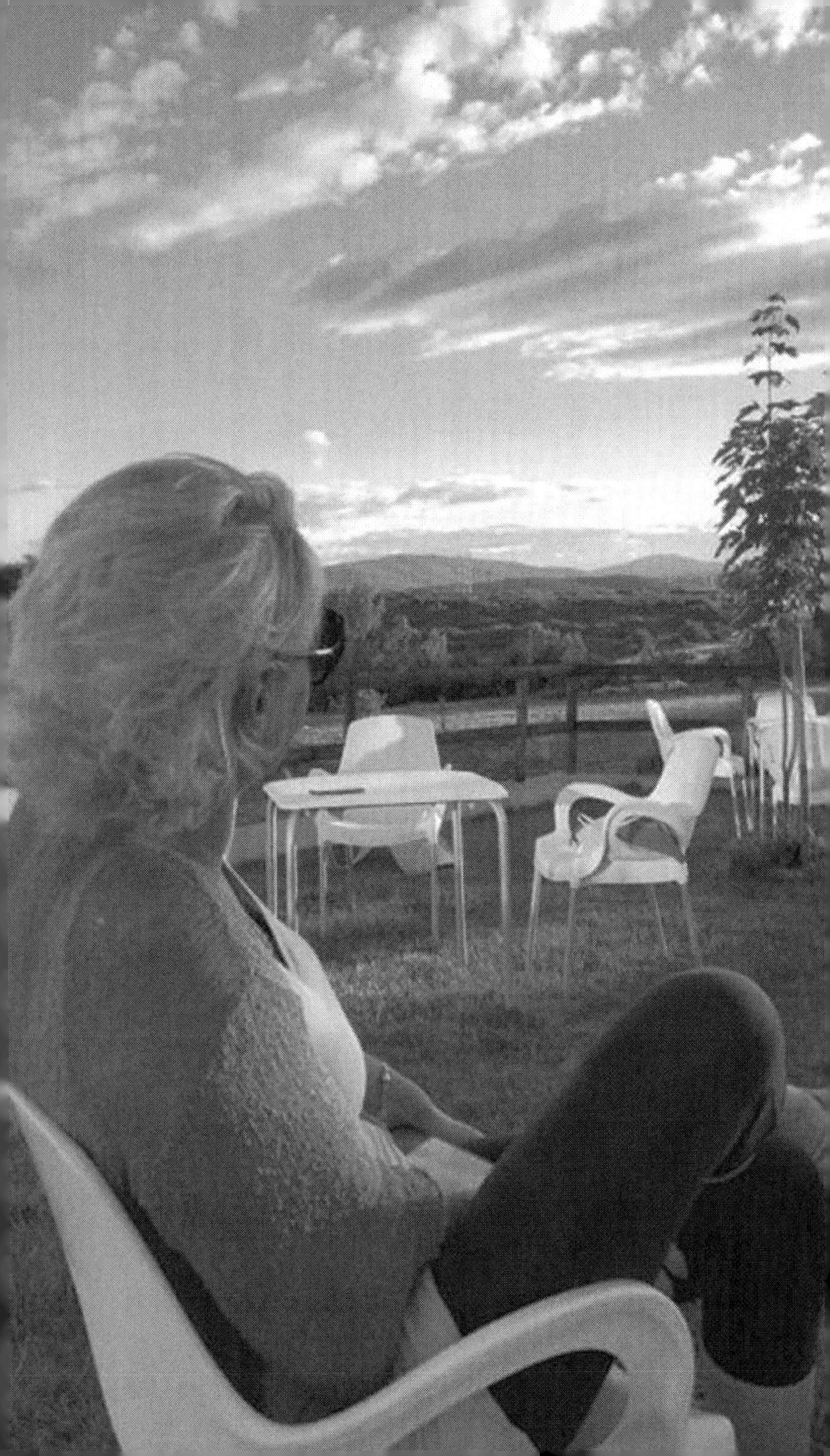

Day Ten

Carrion de Los Condes to Valencia de Don Juan

To rest or not to rest, that is the question

We had been discussing rest days since we sat together that first night in Salles. We had agreed that a couple of rest days or 'easy days' were essential, but up to now we hadn't taken any. Not only had we not rested but we'd had a couple of killer days that ran our energy levels to empty. Up to now, we had recovered reasonably well but every bit of research I'd done told me that rest days are essential. A rest day was on my mind but we needed to get another 100 km under our belts. According to the map, this part of the country was reasonably flat and had decent roads.

We set off on day ten and decided to stop in the first café we came to. It is on the left-hand side as you cycle out of the campsite and up a slight hill, by the church, towards the centre of the town. When you sit outside, you look onto the main, bigger church with two huge stork nests on top of the flat bell tower.

I am giving exact directions because I do not want you to patronise this café, because the owner is the most miserable bastard you will ever come across. There are plastic notices outside, advertising different desayunos - breakfast options. We parked the bikes and walked in and a man with a frown met us. It steadily went from bad to worse to the point where we nearly walked out. Everything was too much trouble for this man; he had clearly never heard of the wise advice given by Confucius around 500 B.C. when he said, "man without smile should not open shop."

He grunted and grumbled about every question we asked and every request we made. At first, I thought it was an anti-foreigner thing, but no, when a young local lad brought in a couple of barrels of beer on a trolley, he didn't manage to get a smile either, nor did he even get a word of response when the lad bid him buenos dias.

I made a point of turning a couple of cyclists away from Grumpy's establishment as they contemplated breakfast and we couldn't wait to get away.

Credit Google Maps

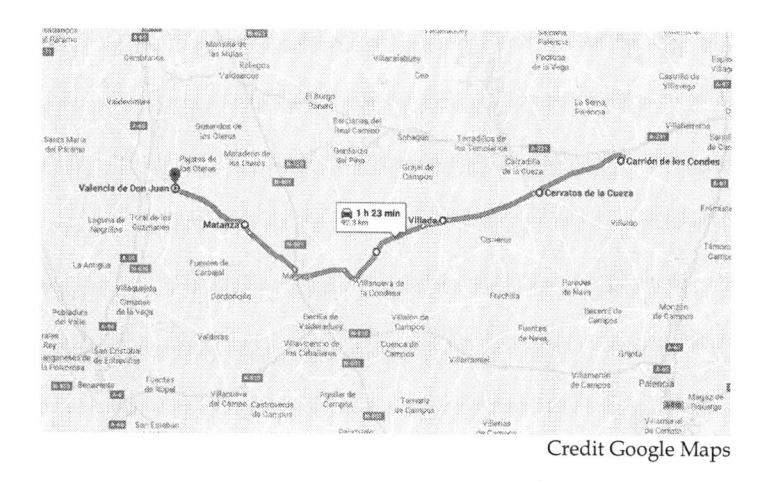

We had one of the easiest mornings we'd had thus far. There was a nice cloud cover, no wind, not even a breeze and we didn't come across a single hill for 25 km. We were back on the N120 which eventually ran onto the P 972 and then the VA 931 to Villagomez La Nuevo.

At lunchtime, (65km) we discussed rest days and we were split into two camps. From a logical point of view, I voted that we add one in and from a practical point of view, Caroline said her backside would benefit from a day off. The lads, however, were in the other camp, Gary saying he didn't need one and Dave saying he hadn't come on the Camino to rest. I tried to reason with them and said if we could ride 100 km today, we would be well ahead of schedule. I had looked at Google Maps and although the next 150 km didn't look overly bad, the terrain around Ponferrada and beyond looked brutal.

I had also calculated the kilometres and told the gang that we had about 100 km to play with, that is, we could take a rest day and spend half a day on a bus or train, pinch a few kilometres, rest, and still achieve our goal of cycling 1,000 kilometres of the Camino de Santiago.

As my Belgian friend had said, everyone has their own idea of their personal Camino and there's nothing wrong with that. Caroline's and my agendas were very much charity motivated as our sponsors had paid up because of the 1,000 Kilometre Challenge. While some hikers wouldn't dream of jumping onto a bus, we met lots of people who took rest days or spent a few hours on a bus or in a taxi because of a niggling injury or just because they felt they were pushing themselves a bit too far. Yet everyone had the same goal at the end of the day and that was to make it to Santiago without dying en route.

If you cycle or walk with a group on the Camino, there will always be disagreements. But without the risk of repeating myself, be warned, always listen to your body and don't risk not making it to Santiago because of a little pride or stubbornness.

And so we cycled on after lunch. I knew that our group was about to split because as much as the boys didn't want to take a rest day, Caroline and I were just as determined to do the sensible thing. It was all about recovery.

Later that afternoon the weather closed in. We had cycled onto a place called Mayorga on the VP 4508 and then turned onto the CL 621 when it started to drizzle. By the time we reached Matanza, it was raining quite hard, but we were in good spirits because we had put in over 90 km.

It was raining gatos and perros by the time we reached Valencia de Don Juan and although there was a four-star campsite in town we knew that we wouldn't be staying there. (Camping Pico Verde) I'm of an age where the days of setting up a tent in the rain are well gone. Apart from anything, everybody's sleeping bag and tent were wet through. We had wrapped everything up, but the rain had been so hard it still managed to get in and soak everything.

We pulled up at the first bar in town. We had completed another 100 km day and all we had to do now was find an apartment or a hotel. Whenever you get to a bar and you haven't got any accommodation always ask. There is always someone who knows someone who has a hotel or a B&B or even an apartment. We asked the barman and he got straight on the phone. We had a few drinks and let him do all the hard work. He was great, the bar is called Taberna Cerveceria Justi, and I highly recommend it. The barman confirmed there were vacancies at a hotel called Villegas.

It was still peeing down, so we had another drink. Now that we had secured some accommodation, we could relax. The menu looked great in the Cerveceria Justi, a lovely restaurant in the back of the bar and we promised the barman we would return as we set off in the rain to find the hotel. We thanked him for all his help.

Unfortunately, we didn't return as it was nearly a kilometre from our hotel and the rain didn't let up. I wish we had though, because we ended up having dinner at the nearest bar and it was awful and grossly overpriced.

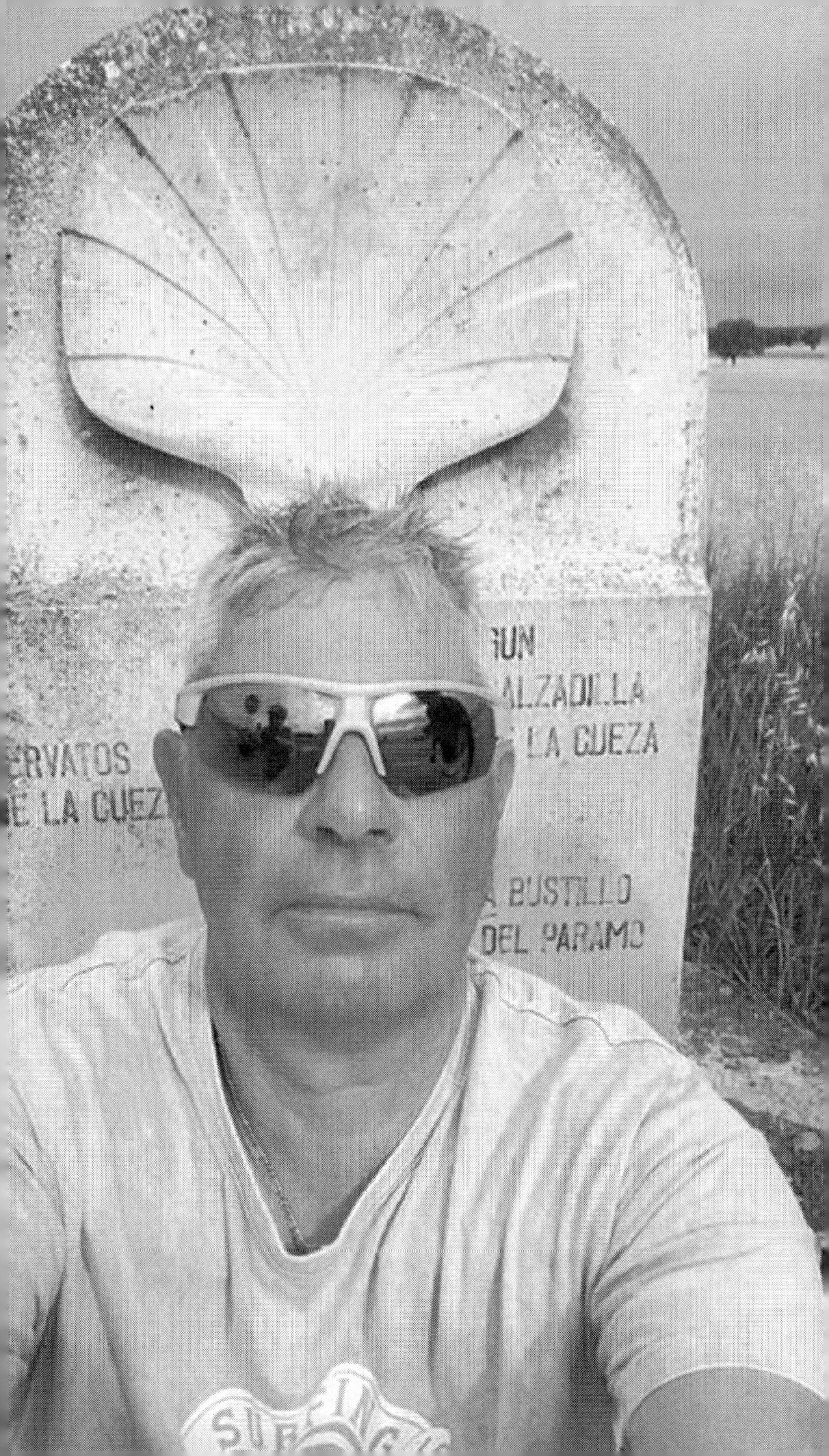
LA CUEZA
BUSTILLO
DEL PARAMO

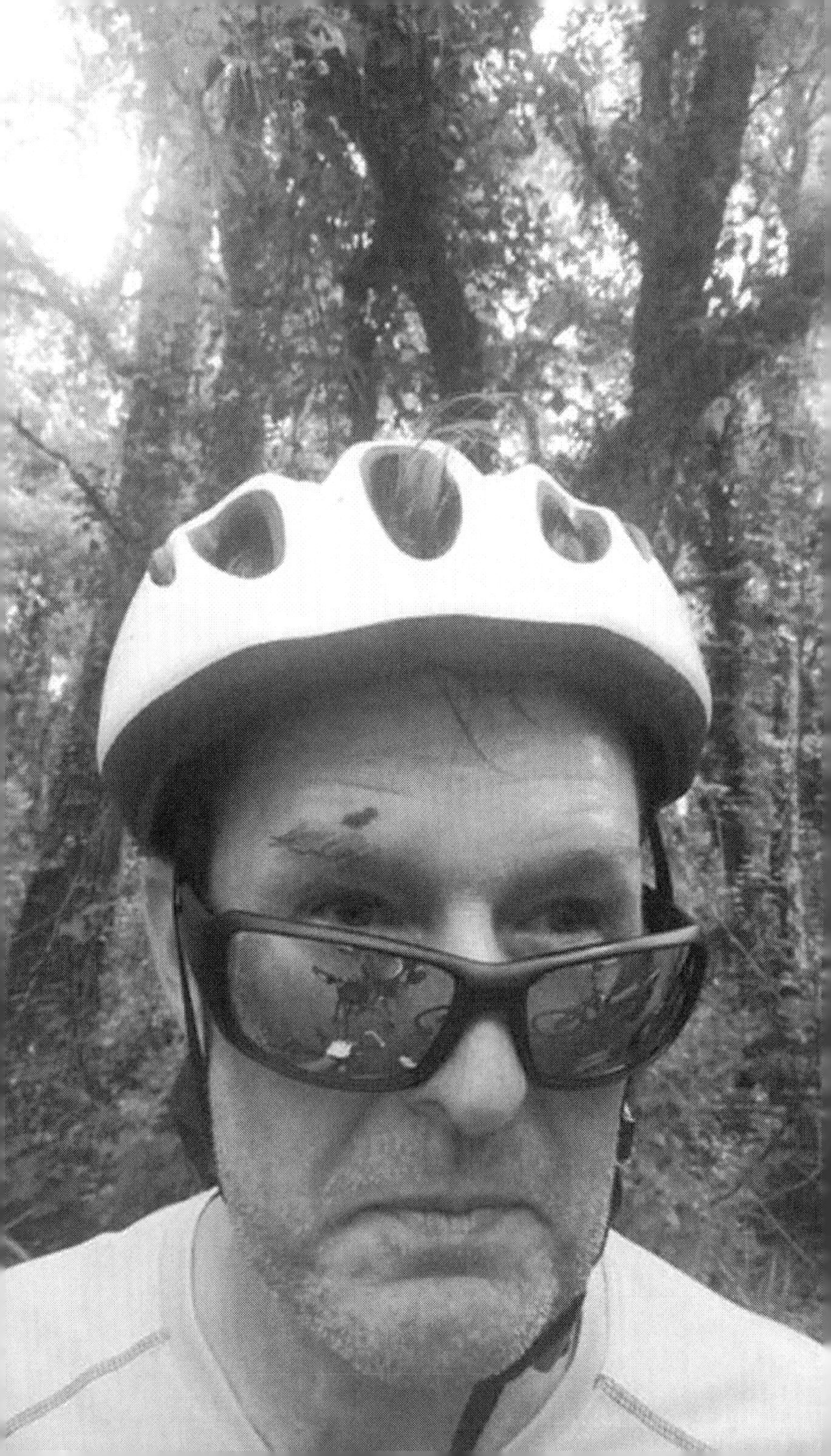

Day Eleven

Valencia de Don Juan to Rabanal del Camino

Ernie, the fastest milkman in the West

It was still raining when we left Hotel Villegas in Valencia de don Juan. We had breakfast in the hotel (it was included in the price) and took some small pastries and fruits which we loaded into our panniers. We probably took a little more than the hotel assumed we could eat in one sitting, but we had learned our lessons, we were on the lookout to steal food wherever we could.

The hotel had a large underbuilt where we had left our bikes and we plotted the route for the day as we loaded them up.

This was now a familiar exercise to us - the more you pack your bike each morning, the easier it becomes. Caroline was really tempted at this point to dump her sleeping bag and tent as she now had no intention of camping. She had researched the Camino too and knew that the nearer we got to Santiago, the more guest houses, hotels and apartments there were.

"What's the point of carting this back to Altea? I'm never going to use it again."

I could tell Caroline was feeling a little like me - invincible. We had broken the back of the challenge, and there was no way we weren't going to achieve what we had set out to achieve.

I think even at this point if I had broken an ankle or a wrist, I would still have soldiered on.

We were less than 350 km from Santiago and we had 70 km in the bank.

I knew where Caroline was coming from, she wanted to enjoy the rest of the journey and if that meant laying out a little more money so she could curl up of a soft mattress then so be it.

The rain eased off after about an hour and the forecast told us it was going to be fair, if not sunny for the rest of the day. By now we were big fans of the Spanish minor roads so there was no need to branch off onto rough cycle paths and everyone was happy.

We were now deep in Camino territory, passing hikers walking by the side of the road every few kilometres. It's a fact, the nearer you get to Santiago the more pilgrims you see and at times, some of the tracks looked quite congested.

The Camino track for the pilgrim walkers ran right alongside the two roads we cycled that morning, the CL621 and the N120 into Astorga. As we approached Astorga around lunchtime the road got a little busier and a whole lot steeper. It was up and down, but mostly up, until we got a couple of kilometres outside Astorga and then it was a pleasant descent into the suburbs.

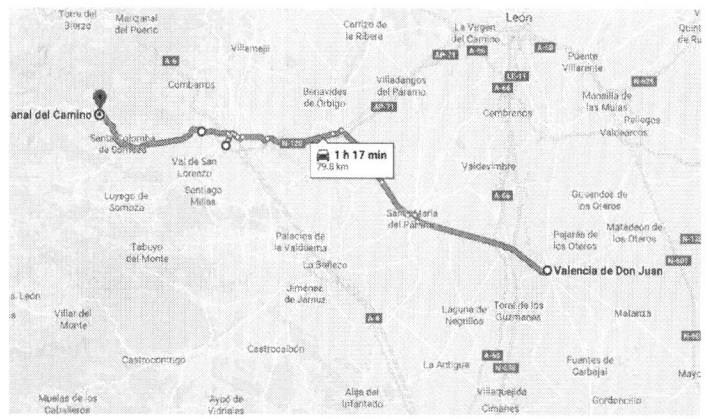

Credit Google Maps

We had made our mind up that we weren't going to do a 100 km day, we were planning to get to a small place called Rabanal del Camino where there were a campsite and a couple of small hotels. That way everybody would be happy.

As we sat down for lunch in a beautiful place on the N120, 2 km from Astorga, the feeling of invincibility was firmly back with us and everyone was in high spirits.

It might have had something to do with where we had stopped for lunch. We'd looked into a couple of places on the left-hand side of the main road, but they looked fairly naff and overpriced and we sensed they were there to exploit the travellers. We didn't want to cycle right into the city of Astorga for obvious reasons; we wanted to skirt the main road if possible.

We were in a small suburb called San Justo de la Vega when we spotted somewhere that we could easily have missed. It was on the right side of the road but slightly set back and if we had been going any faster, we could have missed it. There was a chalkboard outside advertising a menu del día (menu of the day) for 7€. As we parked outside, the owner came out to greet us and beckoned us to bring our bikes into a small courtyard where we chained them up. He then showed us to a table inside and we ordered a drink while we studied the menu. It offered a salad, a choice of pasta or meat dish, a sweet and a drink all for 7€. It was fantastic value and I would highly recommend it, but unfortunately I don't know the name of the establishment and can't find it anywhere on Google.

We chilled out there for two hours and I joined Caroline for a couple of exquisite glasses of wine which were also reasonably priced. Caroline was super organised and decided to book ahead in Rabanal del Camino. She said that single rooms were available at 25€. It sounded too good to be true and I told her to book me one. The lads declined as there was a campsite at Rabanal and that was going to be their spot for the night.

I guessed we were going to regret the two glasses of wine as soon as we set off towards the town. I knew from the map that although we only had about 25 km to go before we reached 'base' there was a fair bit of climbing to do.

It didn't help that we got lost in Astorga. A wonderful place no doubt, but we will remember it for 30 minutes of wasted time and lots of traffic as we looked for signposts that didn't exist.

The town lies at the junction of the French Route and the Via de la Plata route on The Way. There is evidence that Astorga has artefactual evidence stretching back 200,000 years, but the Roman city was officially founded in 14 BC, named by Emperor Octavian as Asturica Augusta, later shortened to Astorga. It was an important administrative and military centre. The walls that you can see to this day are of Roman construction and back in the day the city was one of the most advanced in Europe, it had thermal baths with hot and cold-water systems and even steam rooms and saunas. The Ruins of the Roman baths are still visible today and I´ve heard that it´s worth a visit. There is a legend that Saint James preached in Astorga, perhaps that is why it is such an attraction on The Way.

The city was effectively abandoned during the Moors and Christians conflict, but a century later it was part of the repopulation effort carried out during the reign of Ordoño of Asturias when the city became a major stop on the French route for the pilgrims to the tomb of Saint James. Construction of the cathedral of Astorga began in the 15th century and drew in more pilgrims than ever before. It was the perfect place to rest and get ready to climb the mountains in the west.

This is what I tried to tell Dave and Gary.

"Rest lads," I said, "if it was good enough for the pilgrims of long ago and good enough for the lads on the Tour de France then it's good enough for us."

They wouldn't listen and my pleas fell on deaf ears.

There were two roads out of Astorga both much of a muchness, the LE 6425 and the LE 142. We followed the LE 142 all the way.

Ten kilometres into the last part of the day, the road veered off to the right and narrowed considerably. There was barely room for two cars to pass, but we were in beautiful countryside with the Camino footpath running alongside the road.

It was a tough last part of the journey; up and down the whole way and it was slow going, those extra wines were taking their toll.

Our hostal/hotel was on the left, a hundred metres before the village and what a beautiful spot. Set back a few metres from the road, the single-storey building had several wooden tables outside with a large grassed area to the right where more tables were situated. We walked into the bar, which was also the reception area and the owner Juan, checked us in and asked us what we wanted to drink. There was a chalkboard on the wall advertising bocadillos, tapas, pasta, chicken, steak and fish as well as speciality dishes of the area. Caroline had come up with the goods yet again and I could see the jealousy on the lads' faces.

The lads went outside with their beers while Caroline and I had a quick look at the rooms. Both en suite and spotlessly clean.

As Juan brought a second round of drinks, Dave asked where the village campsite was. Juan said there was no need; the lads could camp on the grass by the hotel free of charge. What a result!

As I have previously mentioned, this happens quite a lot on the Camino. If the owner of an albergue, hostel or hotel realises that you are going to eat and drink there, then they are often quite happy if you camp on their land.

The Hostal La Candela is a highly recommended stopover. You may have to book in advance as they only have about six or seven rooms.

Website: www.hostallacandela.com

Note the spelling of hostal, with an a, and not with an e as we spell it in English.

At around nine o'clock, we asked Juan if we could eat. He said yes but informed us that he only had four main meals to give us as he'd had a busy day and there were minimal supplies on the premises. He had two fish dishes, a spaghetti bolognese and a steak. It wasn't a problem and we quickly decided among ourselves who was having what (Even Dave!).
Be warned, it is quite common that an albergue or hotel can run out of food.

Top Tip. As soon as you arrive at your destination, order your food for the evening. Don't leave it until the last minute or you might go to bed hungry.

After dinner, I got out the maps again, checked the elevation of the route the lads intended to cycle the next day and had one last attempt to talk them out of what was beginning to look like a suicide mission. It equalled the most elevation we had completed in one day during the duration of the challenge and the forecast was for a scorching hot day. They were about to cycle 200 metres higher than the height of Ben Nevis after 11 days in the saddle without a break. I begged them to reconsider but they wouldn't.

Before closing this chapter, you may want to go onto our Facebook group (30 July) and take a look at the video of our night in Rabanal, in the garden area where the lads camped. Dave was a little worse for wear and gave us his version of Benny Hill's, Ernie, the fastest milkman in the west. Let' just say it's worth a look.

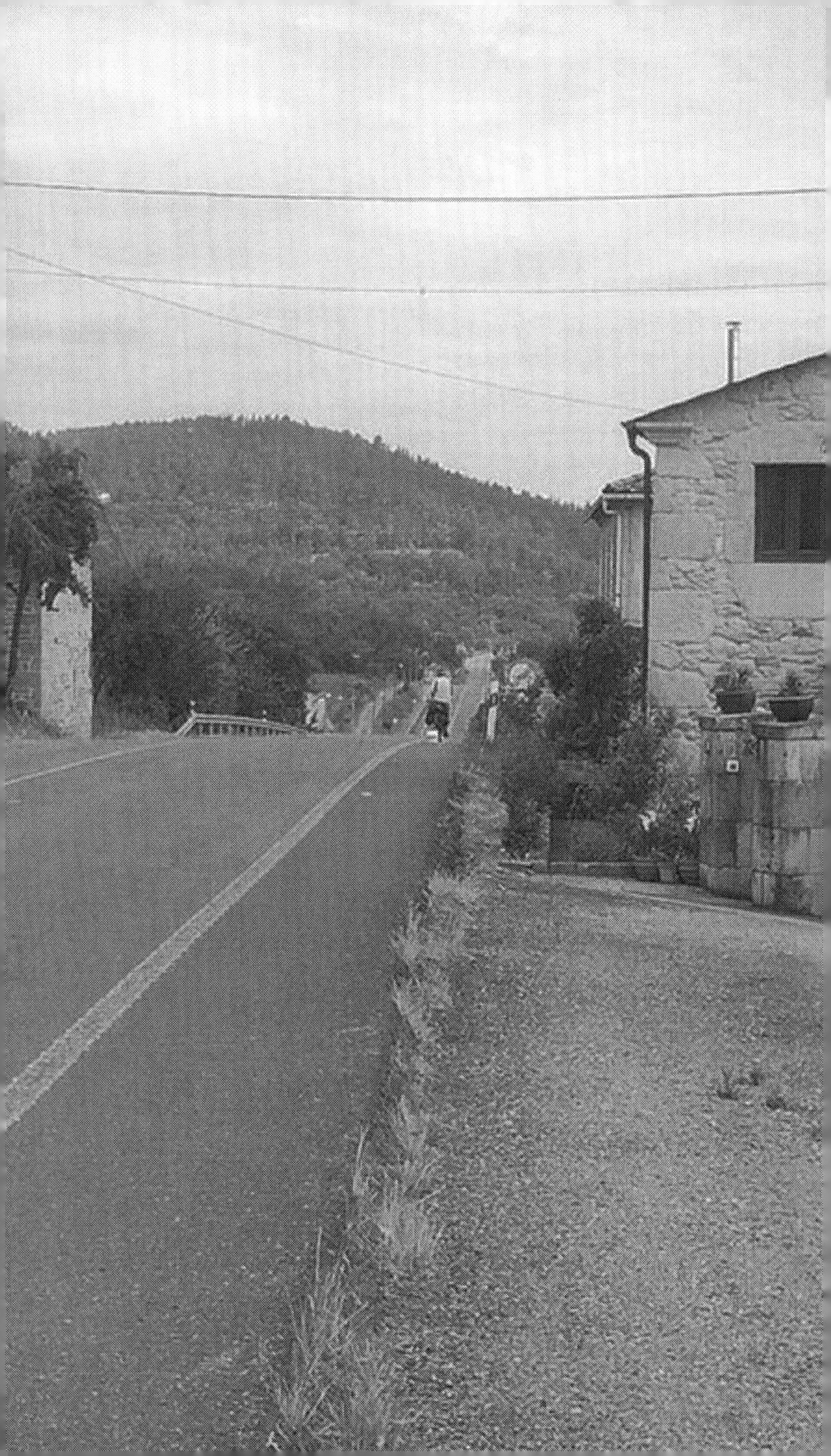

Day Twelve

Rabanal to Pedrafita

The group splits

Dave and Gary set off early, just after breakfast around 7.30 am. I was up and waved them off after sharing a coffee with them. Caroline had a long lie in that day as she was going to make the most of her rest day and I couldn't blame her.
We had planned to meet the boys at a place called Perdrafita de Cebriero.
Although it was only about 60 km as the crow flies, through the mountains, via Ponferrada and a place called La Faba, it was 80 km by road, with a 1,500 metre elevation gain. Google Maps said it was nearly seven hours in the saddle, which told me all I needed to know about what they were going to encounter.

Caroline and I called a minibus transfer company who said they could take us and our bikes to La Faba. We then planned to cycle the short trip to Perdrafita do Cebriero.

The driver would be there at 11.30 am, which gave us enough time to chill out and get ready and drink some more of Juan's coffee. By then, Dave and Gary would have been on the road for four hours.

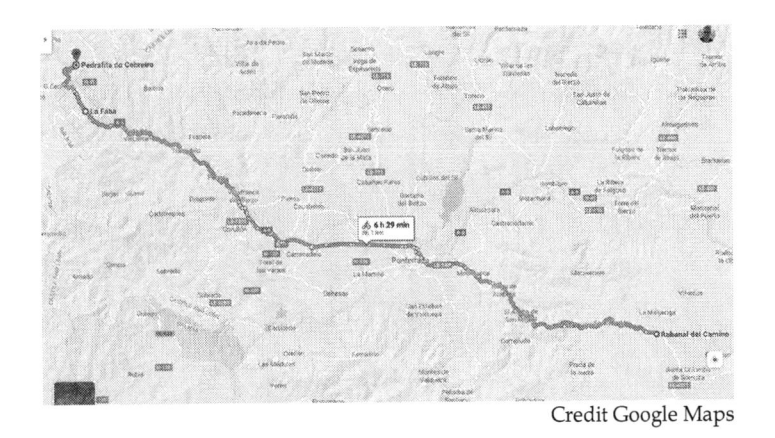

Credit Google Maps

When we set off in the direction of Manjarin, there was an American lady on the bus who was also having a rest day. She was walking the Camino with her husband and had had a few knee issues so rather than risk a complete breakdown she decided to take a taxi to their next intended stopover at Molinaseca while her husband plodded on.

We made it to La Faba by lunchtime and cycled the 4 km to O Cebreiro - a ridiculous elevation of 300 m that took us nearly an hour. Some rest day!!

I wondered how on earth the lads were going to cope with that climb after 70 km in the saddle.

O Cebriero is a gorgeous mountain top hamlet and an iconic stopover on the Camino, and for the first time we were in Galicia, albeit just over the border. The town has two roads leading into it; they are the medieval roads leading to the Camino de Santiago and the Camino Real.

The old homes and buildings are pallozas, buildings that predate Roman times. Many of them have been bought up and restored to provide refuge for pilgrims.

The place was buzzing and Caroline and I parked and enjoyed a beer, but we couldn't help wondering where the boys were.

A little Google research told us the legendary miracle of the Holy Grail occurred in O Cebreiro in the year 1300. Allegedly, during a Holy Mass, a piece of bread turned into flesh and the holy wine in the chalice, turned into blood. The sacred relics of the miracle are guarded near the church where it took place and thousands of pilgrims visit the church every year.

In 1486, the Catholic monarchs, on a pilgrimage to Santiago, stopped at the monastery of O Cebreiro and confirmed that a miracle had indeed taken place 136 years before their visit. The chalice appears on Galicia's coat of Arms.

The road to O Cebreiro played a role in the Spanish wars of Independence owing to its strategic position between León and Galicia. In

1809 it was used by the Scottish troops of John Moore as he retreated to A Coruña with the French in hot pursuit. The French knew how harsh the winter is in that part of the world and they fell back to the lowlands, effectively leaving the British to starve and freeze to death.

You can almost feel the history as you sit in the small square, surrounded by bars, tourist shops and places to stay. We tried a few places to sleep over, but they were all full and there were a lot of American Pilgrims milling around complaining that there was nowhere to stay. The owner of the bar told us that it was one of the most popular places on the Camino and finding accommodation in O Cebriero and Perdrafita do Cebriero was impossible unless you booked several days in advance.

"Are there any campsites nearby?" I asked.

"No."

This was bad news for the lads.

We decided that we needed to head off to try and find accommodation. The rest day was quickly becoming a non-event as we set off in the direction of Perdrafita do Cebriero. We bypassed it and cycled another 9 km to the Albergue Del Puerto on the LU 633 and another steep uphill. We were in business though, they had beds for the night and somewhere to camp. It was our first albergue stop and we decided to try the dorms.

By now it was late afternoon and Caroline and I chilled out at a height of 1,270 m overlooking the valley below. I'm sad to say that, yes, there was alcohol involved again and after a couple of hours I enjoyed a wee siesta in my not so comfortable bed while Caroline baked her body in the sun.

When I woke up, I called the boys to tell them we had reserved their beds for the night. I figured that they deserved a mattress after what they had been through that day. There was no answer.

Caroline and I had skipped lunch, so we ate an early dinner, Galician broth and a meat and potato pie would you believe. Galician fayre is typical of Northern England food and I have to say it was delicious.

As we finished our meal, we eventually got hold of Gary and Dave and it was bad news. They managed about 70 km before they called it a day. Dave's very words were, "I couldn't cycle another ten metres. I'm finished."

We tried to figure out where they were; I think they were a few kilometres short of La Faba, about 17 km away.

They had nowhere to stay as there was no accommodation, no campsites and they were going to set up their tents at the side of the road close to a garage.

I urged them to continue and said there was a bed reserved for them and food too and that it was only a couple of hours away, we couldn't split the group up so close to Santiago. And yet I knew by the sound of his voice it wasn't going to happen.

I resisted the urge to say I told you so and said I would call them the next morning.

I relayed the story to Caroline as we sat in the late evening sunshine. Our bellies were full, we had a very nice bottle of Rioja on the table beside us and a bed for the night, and although we had cycled more kilometres than we had intended to, we were feeling rejuvenated, rested and rather smug. Taking a rest day had been the best decision we had made on the entire trip.

The night was still young and the albergue was filling up, it was quite a good scene. We befriended a lone Irishman called Frank Cullen and a girl from London called Sylvia and we were now the gang of four once more.

I am not a fan of albergues or rather, I am not a fan of their dormitories. The idea of sleeping with a load of farting, coughing and snoring strangers for eight hours of darkness is more than I can bear. This one was worse because it was a mixed dorm, and boy can those girls fart during the night!

However, we had to experience one sleepover at an albergue and this was it. It was an awful night's sleep; give me a one-person tent any day of the week.

What I am a fan of, however, is the pre-sleep ritual.

Everyone knows it's going to be an effort to get to sleep, you are nervous, even a little bit wary (the girls especially, in case they fart too much through the night,) and so most travellers hit the bar in an effort to sink just enough alcohol to numb the senses and yet not too much that it affects your performance the following day.

So, Caroline, me and our two new friends set about our task with gusto. And just when we had sunk enough beers and wine so that it would tip us over to sleep the second we hit the mattress, we started on the brandy.

The one good thing about the albergues is that there is always someone to talk to or with whom to drink a beer. I noticed this from the moment we arrived until the moment we left, I am now a firm fan of albergues, just don't force me to sleep in the dorms.

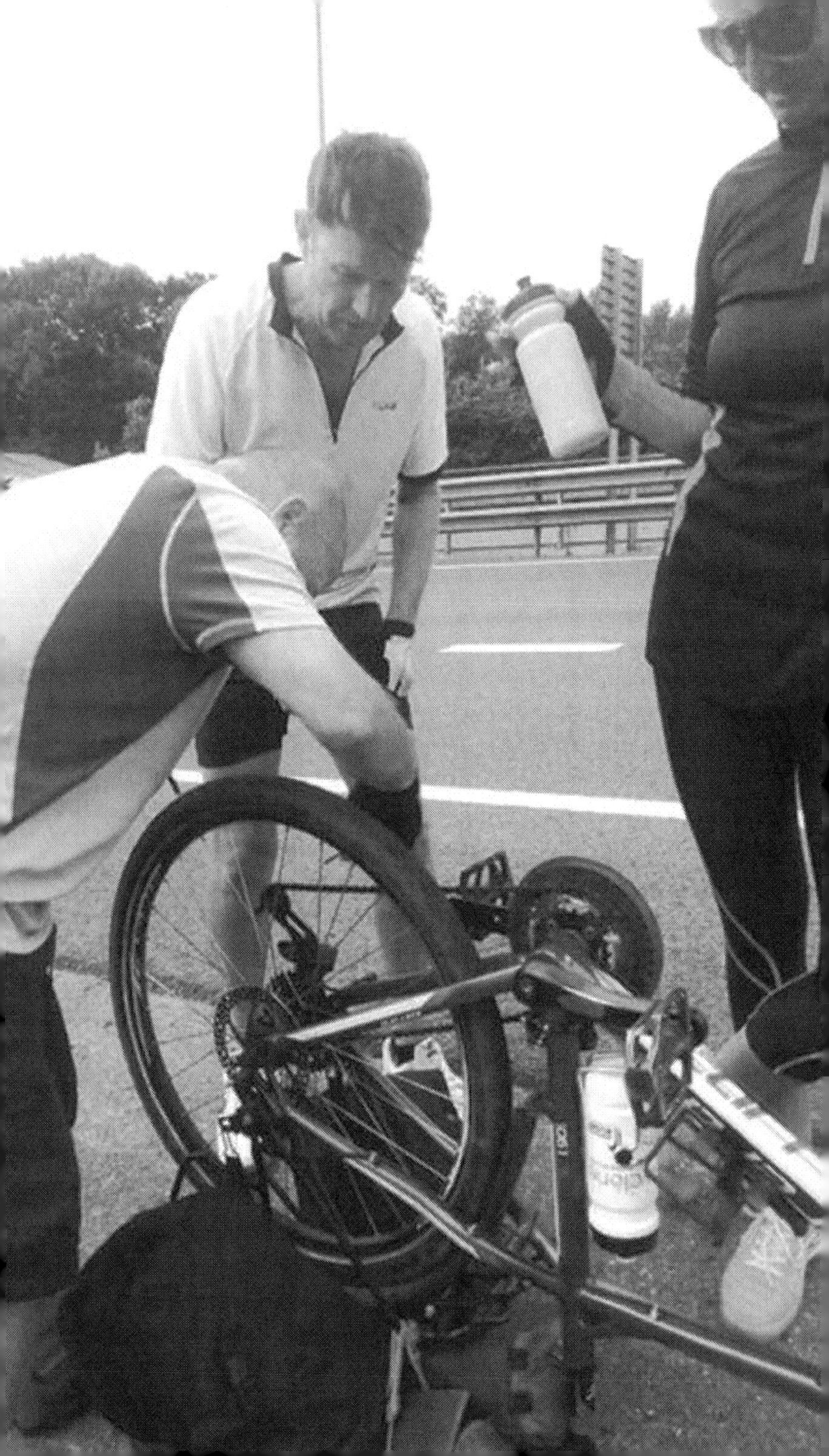

Day Thirteen

Albergue Del Puerto to Palas de Rei

Unlucky for some

We were 175 km from Santiago de Compostela. We couldn't wait to get started, but of course, we had to wait for the boys. I knew from the map that they would have a rough start to the day. I figured they had nearly 600 m of climbing before they reached us and even though it was only around 15 or 16 km, it would take them almost two hours to arrive.

They cycled into the albergue just before ten o'clock. I had timed it perfectly as two plates of bacon and eggs were brought out the moment they pulled up. They attacked their plates with vigour as they told us about the toughest day they'd had on the Camino so far. Once again I resisted the urge to say I told you so and we set off 30 minutes later.

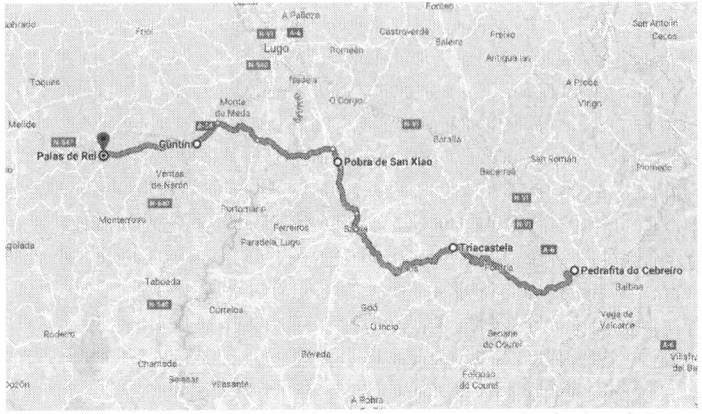

Credit Google Maps

It was downhill all the way, a 700 m descent in 14 km to a place called Triacastella on the LU 633. It was just what the boys needed after their two hours of torture.

We had looked ahead and planned to reach a place called Guntin about 85 km away. It seemed a reasonably sized town with bars and shops and a garage and a hostal. Unfortunately, there was no campsite, but because it was more or less halfway to Santiago, that's where we were laying our heads that night. The only downside was that it was another 700 or 800 metres of climbing. That was on top of the 600 m the lads had already put in before breakfast.

The first part of the day before lunchtime was reasonably kind to us. We followed the LU 633 to

Sarria. It's a great road, hardly any cars and not a pothole to be found anywhere.

The LU 633 led onto the LU 546 and we took lunch in a café on the main road just outside a place called Pobra de San Xiao. We had followed a cycle path at this point and bypassed Pobra de San Xiao completely, but in another few kilometres, like a desert mirage, a charming café appeared out of nowhere.

Over lunch, Dave and Gary came clean. They said that the previous day had been hellish and although they had cycled through some of the most beautiful scenery they had ever seen, they hadn't enjoyed it one bit. They had cycled for 12 days in a row without a break and likened it to a 12 round boxing match, fighting an amateur for 11 rounds and in round 12 they replaced the amateur with Muhammad Ali.

It was the perfect analogy. Caroline and I had also fought the amateur for 11 rounds, but in round 12 they had given us a break and sent us to the corner to rest.

I was enjoying the run that day, Caroline was too, but I could see in their faces that Dave and Gary were in a different place to where we were, and what none of us realised at the time, they were about to put in another killer of a day.

I was quite concerned because some of the research I had done mentioned hitting 'the wall,' when things transition from being pretty hard to being almost impossible. It is the point where your body and mind are simultaneously tested, a combination of fatigue and diminished mental faculties.

It's very real. I ran a few marathons when I was in my twenties and I remember the feeling when you just want to quit, you get disorientated and your mind plays tricks on you. This is because the brain starts directing oxygen to the muscles while other parts of the body are crying out for it.

And we were no spring chickens either, Dave and Gary were 57 years old, or as I kept telling them, 'nearly 60.'

And yet there was nothing we could do. Santiago was now agonisingly close and I knew that we would all get there, it was just sad that they weren't enjoying it as much as we were. As we finished lunch and set off, we were comforted by the fact that Santiago de Compostela was now signposted on the road we were on and we were only 30 km from Guntin.

There were two options from Pobra, the LU P 2904 to Guntin or the LU 613 in the direction of Portomartin. They were much of a muchness and I knew that either route was going to push us to the limit as the last part of the ride was a torturous 450 m climb. We opted for the slightly shorter route towards Crende and about 8 km in, we started to climb.

For 4 km we climbed without respite, it levelled out for 1 km and we climbed again for another 3 km. We took plenty of rests and lots of water. Another steep bit was approaching Crende and suddenly hills were no longer my friends and God knows how the lads were feeling.

I could see signposts for Guntin, only 4 km more and Google Maps told us it was all downhill.

We were elated as we cruised into Guntin. We had made it and no more cycling today.

Or so we thought!

As we breezed into Guntin, I had noticed a hotel on the left-hand side of the road but didn´t pay it much heed because it looked all closed up. We did what we did in most villages and found the nearest bar. Not only do bars serve beer but someone has to serve that beer and more often than not, that person knows just about everything there is to know about the village or town in which they are serving beer.

We ordered the drinks and I asked the girl behind the bar about hotels. She said that the only hotel in town was the one we had passed and it closed its doors some time ago.

"Any other hotels nearby?"

"No."

"Any Casas Rurales?"

"No."

"Any campsites?"

"No."

"Do you know of an apartment for rent?"

"No."

She said the nearest place with accommodation was a village called Palas de Rei, 15 km away.

My heart sank; it was a real kick to the stones. I was exhausted; we had cycled 85 km and the boys had cycled a 100 km without a rest day. How the hell were they going to react to this news?

Dave thought I was joking, but when it was clear that I wasn't, he said that he couldn't cycle another yard and he was just going to pitch his tent by the side of the road. Who was he kidding? I knew him better than he knew himself. Of course he would make it, but I wasn't going to push him just yet.

We stayed at the bar for an hour and Caroline did her wonders with Airbnb. The girl in the bar was right, there wasn't anything nearby, but Caroline secured a house for the night in Palas de Rei and it looked a little bit special.

We researched Palas de Rei and found that there were many restaurants and bars as it's a popular Camino stopover.

We gently coaxed Dave onto his bike with pictures of his bed for the night and details of some of the restaurants in town.

And he made it, of course, he did.

I was wrecked when we arrived and I couldn't begin to think how Gary and Dave felt as they had cycled another 115 km on top of their day from hell the previous day. Dave's feat of endurance and pushing himself through yet another wall was especially impressive given what he had been through over the last 12 months with his cancer scare.

We had a house all to ourselves, a four-bedroomed detached house in its own grounds. It was stunning. If we'd had some food and beer,

I'm sure we would have collapsed and stayed there that night, but we didn't.

We showered and changed and then took a taxi into town. Once the first beer and forkful of food had passed our lips, the trials and tribulations of the day were all forgotten and we focussed on our final day.

We were in high spirits and because we had pushed on another 15 km, it was only 70 km to Santiago.

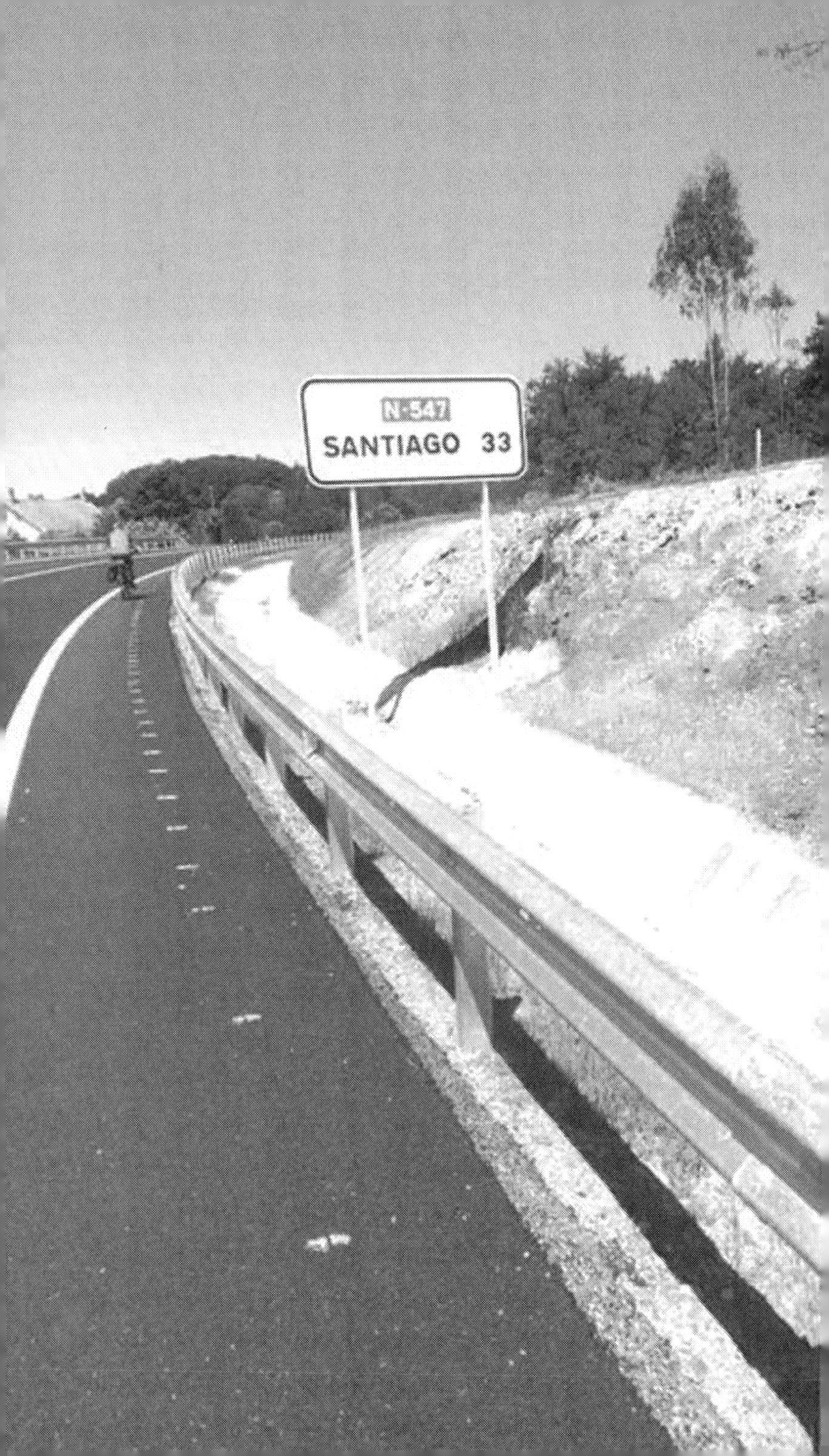
N-547
SANTIAGO 33

Day Fourteen

Palas de Rei to Santiago de Campostela

The road to Santiago

It was the last day and we didn't plan to get up too early, however by the time I made it out of bed, Dave and Caroline had been up a while trying to sort out how we were all going to get home.
It was about the only thing I hadn't planned because I didn't know that all four of us would make it to Santiago in one piece and furthermore, even though we scheduled each day, we didn't know the exact day we would arrive in the city. As it happened, we were going to arrive 24 hours ahead of schedule; a fantastic effort.

There is an airport, a bus station and a train station in Santiago so I couldn't foresee any real problems in making it home.

My idea was to cycle into town and spend a day or two exploring Santiago and arrange things when we got there.

Now it appeared that Dave was desperate to get back to the UK. I wonder if it may have been something to do with the last two days, he had suffered badly.

Gary, as always, wasn't bothered in the slightest; he was the 'whatever man,' but he had five days to play with before he had to get back to work, so he was in no hurry either.

I realised that we all had different agendas. Before we left that morning, Dave and Gary were looking to book onto an early morning flight back to Newcastle the following day, Caroline was considering a midday flight back to Alicante and I wanted to hang around in Santiago for a day or two.

I won't hide my disappointment as I had a very clear picture of what it should have been like in Santiago. It was the very culmination of our cycle challenge and not only should we be celebrating the fact that we had achieved such a remarkable undertaking, but it was the first time in 14 days that we would be able to relax and spend some time together as amigos. We could party till the early hours without worrying about the next day's kilometres and could spend the following day on the tourist trail.

Unfortunately, it didn´t happen like that.

Credit Google Maps

We saw the Santiago de Compostela signposts as soon as we hit the road out of town. It was the only inspiration we needed. It was going to be a hot day, but nowhere near the kilometres we had put in on previous days. We were to follow the N547 most of the day and we weren't going to get lost.

It was a strange feeling knowing that this was to be our final day together and as I cycled along, I sensed that I was going to miss getting up in the mornings and the friendly banter and setting off into the great unknown. We didn't know the roads, or where we were going to eat and we didn't know whether our bodies and our bikes would hold out. Furthermore, some nights we didn't know where we were even going to sleep. That was the fun of it all. We are all governed by time and schedules and we are all caught up in the rat race. I keep saying this, but this isn't everyone's idea of a holiday.

Many pilgrims on The Way are just out for a hike or a spiritual experience. Others are there to find themselves and to get away from it all. It's a chance to say bollocks to the world and walk until you can walk no more. With the cyclist, it's the same. And if you are lucky enough to get a hot meal and a bed for the night, then it's a bonus.

For some, it's the riskiest thing they've ever done with their lives and even though it can frighten the hell out of them, they love the fact that they dared to take on the challenge. It takes a certain amount of bravery to head off to a foreign country with no idea where you are going to get to or where you are going to sleep at night.

Frank Cullen, who I mentioned earlier, was one of the characters I warmed to immediately because it was his first night on the Camino and, not only did he not know where he was sleeping that night, he didn't know where he was walking to the next day. Love it!

Someone asked him how far he intended to walk each day and he just smiled and shrugged his shoulders.

"But where are you aiming for tomorrow?"

Frank shrugged his shoulders again.

"But you must have an idea of how long it will take you to get to Santiago."

Frank shrugged his shoulders again.

Frank didn't even have a tent or a guidebook or a map; he simply didn't care. Frank Cullen and Jan Vandersypen were my two heroes of the Camino because they were doing it exactly how it should be done. Jan said he never booked ahead and had only failed to get a bed for the night once. He has been walking and cycling the Camino for 22 years. By definition, I'm a people watcher; after all, it goes with the job. I can almost always sum up a person soon after meeting them, particularly over a beer or two and I sensed there was a reason why Frank was walking The Way. At around midnight, I found out why. Frank emailed me when we both returned home because I asked him for a few paragraphs on his Camino experience.

This is what he wrote and he sums it up well: I think there are a lot of people on the Camino like Frank.

I was captivated from start to finish by the whole Camino experience. The scenery in the mountains and woodlands of Galicia was nothing short of breathtaking. Coming from Ireland, I was also struck by the remarkable similarities, not only in the landscape but also in the people, who, like the Irish, are of Celtic origin. I spent eight glorious days (25 June to 4 July 2019) hiking the Camino Frances, from O Cebreiro to Santiago, a distance of 161 km. I had known about the Camino from years back, and while I had always thought it was something I would love to do, for a variety of reasons, I had not yet got around to it. Among many things, the Camino was a journey of reflection for me. My wife, Paula, passed away in 2012 from cancer, and my son was away on his first holiday abroad, so when I found myself with this window of time, I donned the rucksack, threw caution to the wind, and away I went!

I had no real tangible reason for going; it was more an adventure, a time to get to know myself, on my own, for the first time in almost 30 years. As well as a reflection on the past and the future, it was also a journey of discovery for me, during which I met many interesting people with fascinating stories to tell. Some were strange, some funny, some even eccentric, but all were very friendly and willing to share their own thoughts among friends; and the conversations along the road, and over a beer or glass of vino in the evening, were one of the highlights of my Camino. The other highlight was, of course, the unspoilt landscape of north-western Spain. I've always had a thing for Spain going back many years and many visits, where I enjoy nothing more than practising my "poco Espanol" with the locals whenever the opportunity arises. This, however, was my first time to see Galicia and I just fell in love with the place there and then. I loved the early morning starts, on with the rucksack and off into the hills. The sights, sounds and smells of the rustic unspoilt countryside were something to behold. Following ancient pathways through tumbledown villages and farmyards, while listening to the birds singing, cows mooing, and cocks crowing was magical; enriched even further by the faint sound of distant cowbells tinkling across the lush green valleys. Just me and the old country, I loved it, my senses stimulated by the aromatic fragrance of pines and lavender, brought back down to earth with the thick fresh smell of good old-fashioned manure. Nothing like it!

I felt myself getting sad the nearer I got to Santiago for the simple reason that I did not want this journey to end so soon. Before reaching Santiago, I had already made up my mind that this is the first of many Caminos for me. Next time I plan to start at the beginning in Saint-Jean-Pied-de-Port, in the company of my son, and it can't come quickly enough!

I guess it was a day of reflection for all of us and I noticed that we cycled with some distance between us on that final day. As we stopped along the way, more arrangements were being made to get home. We made stops for breakfast, coffee and lunch and Caroline and Dave were constantly on their phones making final arrangements. This wasn't how I had envisaged our last day.

At this point in the day, I confess I was dismayed because Dave was now talking about not even spending a night in Santiago. The flight was at 6.00 am and they had to be there two hours before, so he wasn't going to bother with a hotel for the night. They would have something to eat in Santiago when we arrived and then head straight to the airport and sleep there on the airport seats. They were planning to spend no more than three or four hours in the city.

That was utterly ridiculous and I told him so.

"It's not the way to spend our last night together."

"I just want to get home Scotty," he said.

I remembered the scene from Martin Sheen's movie, The Way, when the amigos all eventually made it to Santiago. They'd roughed and bummed

along the pilgrimage together; they'd had their disagreements and fights, their ups and downs. This is what the Camino is all about. We had done the same. But when Sheen's character, Tom Avery, walked into the city of Santiago and he knew that he had completed what he set out to do, he decided to give his companions a little treat and booked them all individual suites in the best hotel in the city. It's a fantastic scene, a real feel-good part of the film.
While I wasn't going to book our gang into the best place in Santiago, I did want to do something special the night we rolled into town.

We had lunch just past a place called O Pedrouzo. It was full of pilgrims and we knew how close we were. We passed the signs for Santiago every six or seven kilometres and we took photographs and went live on Facebook so that our sponsors could see how close we were.
We stopped at a bar near Santiago Airport, which is about 12 km from the city. Dave and Gary called the airport to make sure they offered a 'box-up-your-bike-service', and it was good news, they did.

Top Tip. If you are flying from Santiago Airport, there is no need to dismantle your bike. For 19€ they will do it all for you and box it up.

But be warned, the airport is quite a way out from the city and it's quite high in elevation. Give yourselves a couple of hours if you intend to cycle from the city out to the airport.

We stopped at the first road sign of the city boundary. We had our photographs taken. We made it! Did we feel good? You bet we did, it's something that you can't really describe and after ten minutes of back slapping and congratulations we set off on the final two kilometres to find the Cathedral of Santiago, the iconic finishing post of The Way.

It was weird standing in front of the enormous cathedral, knowing that we had arrived at our final destination. Even though I am not a religious person, it was quite an emotional moment; one can't help but be impressed. I took a video of Caroline as she crouched down beside her bike in front of the huge iconic facade. It looks as if she can't move and I expected her to burst into tears, but she held her composure well. (It's on the Facebook group, 28 June)

There was, however, someone crying their eyes out, a young girl about 20 years of age. She wailed and sobbed as she looked up at the cathedral and one or two of her friends were trying to console her. They had clearly walked The Way, and it was all too much for her. Dave thought she was an attention-seeker, and he was probably right, I thought to myself as I heard her tell one of her friends how awesome it all was.

The cathedral is one of the only three known churches in the world built over the tomb of an apostle of Jesus. The other two are in The Vatican and Chennai in India. However, heed my previous warning of religious legends. If you are a devout Catholic or of a pious nature, I probably shouldn't tell you that the Romans persecuted Spanish Christians in the 3rd century and the original church built to house the tomb of St James was razed to the ground and his resting place abandoned and lost. But don't worry, according to legend, his tomb was rediscovered 600 years later by the hermit, Pelagius, after he witnessed strange lights in the night sky.

The Bishop Theodore of Iria called it a miracle and informed the king who subsequently ordered the construction of a chapel on the site.

But St James still couldn't rest in peace. By another twist of fate, during the Moors and Christians wars, the chapel was attacked by the Muslims in 997 and reduced to ashes. However, legend once again tells us that St James' tomb and the relics were left undisturbed.

Napoleon also sacked Santiago during the Napoleonic Wars and once again St James' remains were lost for another century before being miraculously rediscovered. One thing you can say about Saint James; even after his death he had quite a few miracles up the sleeve of his shroud.

Construction of the present, mostly granite Cathedral, began in 1075 and the last stone was laid in 1122, but the cathedral certainly wasn't finished. For example, the Baroque façade that you see today was completed in 1740, but stonemasons work on the structure even today.

It is the largest Romanesque church in Spain and even this atheist can't help but look up in awe of the magnificent structure. But I wonder how many Spanish peasants lost their lives working on the·cathedral during the construction, or how many families went hungry as a result of much-needed money being directed to the cause.

We spent 30 or 40 minutes in the square, taking pictures and chatting. We held our bikes above our heads which is customary for a cyclist who makes it to Santiago. Again, you can see those photographs and videos on our Facebook group. We found a bar just off the square where we could still view and take pictures of the cathedral. It was ridiculously expensive as you can imagine, but for once we didn't care. We had a few hours left with the lads and we weren't going to waste it looking around for a cheap bar.

The time flew far too quickly and the lads climbed into a taxi and left for the airport.

Caroline had booked a hotel in Santiago for the night and we called a taxi too, as we were in no fit state to cycle there.

The taxi driver had never heard of the hotel. Caroline showed him the Airbnb reservation and he started to laugh. She had booked a hotel in Santiago in Chile.

However, he took us to another hotel on the other side of the city that belonged to his friend. It was way off the tourist track but still quite expensive and not in the best part of town. We checked in, showered, changed and went out. We managed to find a few bars, but none of them served any food; all the kitchens were closed. Around midnight we called it a day and went back to the hotel.

The lads were gone, we hadn't even eaten and it was a disappointing anti-climax to what should have been a spectacular final night.

The following morning, we had an early breakfast and wandered back to the main square. We couldn't believe our eyes as we bumped into Jan Vandersypen. He had made it again, year 23 on the Camino. We had coffee and brandies with him but couldn't stay too long as Caroline had a taxi booked for the airport and I had to disassemble her bike. After I waved her off, I climbed on my bike and cycled back to the city on my own.

I mooched around, visited a few parks, the Pazo de Raxoi, the 12th-century church of Santa Maria and had a few drinks in some of the bars away from the main square.

By late afternoon I knew I had to arrange a bed for the evening because I quite fancied a night out at a decent restaurant as a final farewell. I also had to look at getting home.

My Google search took me to a campsite just two kilometres from Santiago Cathedral and it even had a swimming pool; a place called 'As Cancelas.' Perfect!

Now I just needed to find out how I was going to get home. Tomorrow was Sunday which can be a tricky day to find transport. Then again, if I had to leave on Monday, it wasn't the end of the world.

I cycled to the bus station to enquire about late afternoon buses. My wife had already checked on the Spanish Alsa buses and said they were cheap and regular and bikes were not a problem.

I cycled up to the window and enquired about buses to Alicante. It was the beginning of the Spanish summer holidays that weekend and the girl told me that the coaches on Sunday were all full. Monday was fine and I'd have my choice of buses that left every few hours. She pointed to the clock above her and told me there was a bus leaving in a couple of hours, and there were plenty of seats still available on Saturday's buses.

I said no at first because I wanted to see more of the city and stay at least one more night. But in the end, it was too much of a temptation knowing that I would be back home at six o'clock the following morning. I returned to the window and booked my ticket.

As I've already stated, Santiago is a major city and whatever part of the globe you have come from you won't have any trouble getting home.

Caroline and the lads had paid a lot of money for their flights back home, and in hindsight, it would have been wise to book in advance as it would have been so much cheaper. But it's easy to say that after we all made it safely to Santiago and ahead of schedule.

The Practicalities

I do hope you enjoyed part one of this book and that it may have spurred you on to believe that cycling at least a part of the Camino is certainly within your capabilities.
Part Two of this book is quite simply entitled *The Practicalities*, because as you are no doubt aware now, (after reading part one,) a successful expedition on the Camino takes a lot of planning and the group leader, in this case, me, must also ensure that his travelling companions are aware of just what is required of them. If you are cycling as a group, I suggest you create a Facebook and WhatsApp group, that way critical information can be shared. That way there are no excuses for one of your number turning up without spare

tubes and additional water bottles. A top tip here, spread your tool kit among your group, there's no need for every member of your party to carry a pump, spanners, alan keys, wrenches, a mallet, first aid kit etc. Talk to each other; it's all about making your bike as light as possible.

The last part of this book is Ken Scott's overall take on our grand adventure. And, if you have enjoyed our adventure and have the urge to look at doing it, then there's some good news for you, because we intend to do this all again, but this time correctly.

See page 228 for details of our upcoming challenges.

But first, let's go back in time.

The History of the Camino de Santiago

The Camino de Santiago, or The Way, follows many routes from different countries that ultimately lead to the shrine of the apostle Saint James, at Santiago de Compostela.

It was originally dreamt up in the Middle Ages as a pilgrimage route on which pilgrims could earn indulgences from the Church. Pilgrims originally saw it as both a punishment as well as a time to reflect on their sins. The Catholic Church fixates on sin even to this day. We are born in sin, they say; we sin throughout our lives, and we must pay for those sins. I'm not sure of the Bishop or

Archbishop or perhaps even the Pope who came up with this penance, but originally the 'sinner' was made to walk from Rome to Santiago de Compostela, a mere 2,200 km.

It's also worth bearing in mind that there was a distinct lack of public transport back in the Middle ages so most of the sinners who made it to Santiago de Compostela had no option but to enjoy a swift beer in the local inn, turn around, and set off back to Rome. That original route from Rome passed through Saint-Jean-Pied-de-Port and over time even the Popes and Cardinals of the time thought that walking from Rome was a bit harsh so the traditional starting point of the Camino Pilgrimage was born and started from the Basque village in the Pyrenees.

The pueblo, or Commune of Saint-Jean-Pied-de-Port is a beautiful place, it's worth the climbing that you will endure just for the visit, a Basque town with mainly sandstone buildings just 5 km from the French border. But a warning, plan your cycle route well, it's not the ideal start to the Camino. Cycling the 78 km to Leitza from Saint-Jean-Pied-de-Port is an ascent of 1,417 metres, that's slightly higher than Ben Nevis.

The trick is to take it easy at the beginning, don't kill yourself. Start the day early, take plenty rests and fill those water bottles whenever you can. I met one group of elderly cyclists (60 plus) who were quite happy to take a minibus for the first 20 km making it a more manageable 58 km climb. It was still a tough day and it's not cheating if it helps you complete your goal at the end of the journey, which is to make it to Santiago de Compostela in one piece.

I have already stated the importance of rest days. Two of our group flatly refused to take any rest days and they nearly paid the price.

Anyway, back to your history lesson. St James was one of the disciples of Jesus and it is written that he may have even been the cousin of Jesus himself. James was a fisherman; he was there when Jesus called on him to be a "fisher of men."

Unfortunately, Saint James was beheaded by King Herod, because apparently he wasn't the saint he's made out to be. He had a foul temper and was known as one of 'the sons of Thunder.'

It is written that this foul temper led to his eventual downfall. King Herod, trying to reason with him, was at the end of his tether and eventually ordered his execution.

Saint James was once rebuked by Jesus for demanding that God consume a certain Samaritan town with fire because the residents had upset him in some way. Don't tell the pilgrims, but St James seemed like a nasty piece of work to me.

His head, after his execution was buried under an altar in Jerusalem and the rest of his remains were shipped to the cathedral at Santiago de Compostela, or so the legend goes. Paying homage to Saint James is the reason why many pilgrims walk and cycle The Way.

While the traditional and most popular route

starts from Saint-Jean-Pied-de-Port there are now over a dozen recognised routes and hundreds more that are well established but not officially marked with route markers. Some of the newer routes are off the beaten track and they don't have easy access to hotels and *albergues* etc.

I mention this in previous chapters but it is always wise to carry a lightweight tent or 'bivvy bag' if you are straying off the traditional routes. There's nothing worse than not having a place to lay your head after a tough day on the Camino.

It really is incredible how old these pilgrimages are. Every turn of your wheel or step with your walking boot you are recreating a part of history. The earliest records start in the middle of the 11th century and in the 12th century it was documented that large numbers of foreign pilgrims were journeying from abroad to tread the way of Saint James. And you thought Thomas Cook started the tourism revolution! The routes were well trodden during the Middle Ages but the Black Death and political unrest during the 16th century led to a decline of pilgrims.

In October 1987, the Camino was declared the first European Cultural route and the gateway to the city of Santiago de Compostela was declared a UNESCO world heritage Site. I think the movie The Way, starring Martin Sheen, catapulted the Camino de Santiago into a different stratosphere and since the premiere of that fantastic film, the amount of pilgrims year on year is increasing by over twenty thousand as more and more people want to experience the Camino and head back home with wondrous tales of physical endurance, fulfilment and inner peace. It seems that every man and his dog now wants a piece of the action.

The main route to Santiago follows an old Roman trade route. It traditionally ends on Galicia's Atlantic coast, ending at Cape Finisterre. The Romans named the town of Finisterrae, which literally translated means *the end of the world.*

The scallop shell, which you will see hanging from a thousand rucksacks during your time on the Camino is found on the shores of Galicia. There are several explanations why the scallop shell has become a symbol of the Camino. Many say it is as simple as taking home a souvenir of Galicia but in days gone by it was said that the shell was a perfect tool to take on the trail as it's the right size to take up a scoop of water from a well or to eat from a bowl of food. During the middle ages, taking a scallop shell back to Rome was seen as proof that the pilgrim had made it all the way to Galicia. You may be lucky enough to gather up a scallop shell en route. If you look carefully, they are there to be found. Paying 3 or 4€ from a street vendor or a shop is a guaranteed way of getting your souvenir but remember, traditionally the 'badge' of completion was always awarded at the end of the Camino.

If you make it to Santiago de Compostela and intend to continue on to the Atlantic coast, to Fisterra or Noia or Muros (two shorter routes to the Atlantic coast,) you will find scallop shells by the hundreds.

There is one other theory behind the scallop shell and one that I like. They say that the shell is metaphor of the Camino, because all of the grooves come to one defined point representing the many paths and starting points of the Camino which eventually come together at Santiago. That is beautiful and so true and will do for me.

A lot of travellers feel the need to trek or cycle the additional 80 km to Fisterra as tradition has it that it is the most western point of the Iberian Atlantic Coast.

Don't tell anyone, but it isn't. A certain town in Portugal takes that distinction. If you really feel the need to see the Atlantic Ocean at the end of your journey, consider heading for Caldebarcos or even Noia or Tavilo. You'll find them on the map and after the sheer effort of just getting to Santiago it's worth considering the shorter routes.

The Camino has become an enormous commercial phenomenon, not necessarily a bad thing at times, because most of the organisations along the way are there to help make your pilgrimage as pleasant as possible. From *albergues* to transportation companies, taxis and guides it is no longer the punishment it was originally intended to be.

As far back as the Middle Ages, there were people along The Way set up to meet the daily needs of pilgrims on their way to and from Santiago de

Compostela. There were hospitals set up to care for injured pilgrims and some Spanish towns still bear the name to this day, for example Hospital de Orbigo. The hospitals, often just a small pueblo with three or four buildings were originally staffed by Catholic nuns. Of course, the nuns insisted that all treatment, not to mention food and lodgings had to be paid for but many of the poorer pilgrims had very little money. The Church therefore decided that anyone who could not pay had to embark on a system of rituals, known as penance. There are ambiguities on just what these forms of punishment were, but more often than not the pilgrims were made to carry rocks in their packs, or an extra 100 miles would be tagged onto their journey.

The rocks-in-the-packs punishment cannot be disputed as it is well documented in many Catholic Encyclopaedias and reference books. Indeed, there is still a tradition in Flanders of pardoning and releasing one prisoner every year under the condition that the prisoner walks to Santiago wearing a heavy backpack.

As I researched this chapter, I had to laugh at some of the references that came up about Saint James. Bearing in mind he was purported to be one of Jesus's disciples, I almost fell off my seat when I read that it was documented that Saint James took part in the final battle that drove the Moors from Spain, he fought gallantly and I quote "with a drawn sword at the head of the Spanish troops, on horseback."

It was quite an achievement on his behalf as the Moors weren't driven out of Spain until 1492. That would have made Saint James over 1,500 years old. But why let mere facts stand in the way of a good legend?

The Spanish people sincerely believed that they owed that victory to Saint James the Apostle and vowed to pay homage to him forever more. And they did, they still do.

The Camino saw an explosion of Pilgrims after the Moors were driven from the Iberian Peninsula. The Middle Ages were a golden period for pilgrims and in modern times it seems that the pilgrimage of Saint James was supported by the Spanish government of Francisco Franco. Franco promoted the route and encouraged more pilgrims than ever before. It was a celebration of 'Spain's Catholic history', he said and the numbers steadily increased in the fifties, sixties and seventies.

Only since the 1990s has the pilgrimage to Santiago regained the popularity it once had in the Middle Ages.

Since then, millions of walkers and cyclists and even pilgrims on donkeys have completed their own individual Camino and ended up at the Cathedral of Santiago de Compostela.

In 2018, it was noted that over 300,000, pilgrims set out to complete the Camino. Some came from the traditional starting points across Europe, but many travelled from the America's and Asia, and for some strange reason the Koreans are now travelling in their thousands. We met dozens of Korean families during our trip, mothers and fathers walking with their children and groups of students eager to experience, The Way, though we didn't meet any fellow Korean cyclists for some strange reason.

The Routes

I am acutely aware of the different capabilities of cyclists and this book gives the cyclist several options and detailed routes. These range from a tough 14-day, 1,100 km challenge from Bordeaux to Santiago de Compostela, to a more genteel, but still challenging, five-day, 285 km cycle from Astorga. I have detailed some of the possible stopovers on these routes, the daily kilometres and alternative routes that may cut out some elevation. The reality is that there is a route for every level of cyclist from the novice to the expert. And remember, you don't have to do it in 14 days like we did. Take 16, or 18 days. Add in more rest days or ride shorter distances each day. Remember, the kilometres you average each day is your choice and you should base it on of the capabilities of the slowest member in your group.

Route 1

Bordeaux via Irun to Santiago de Compostela

1,100 kilometres

Detailed in Chapters 1 to 14

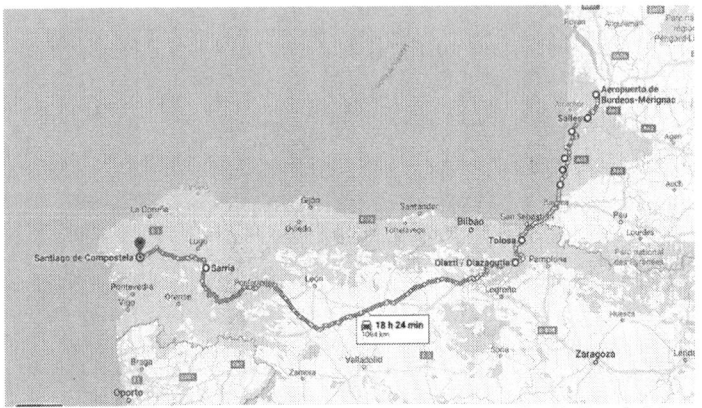

Credit Google Maps

Route 2

Bordeaux via Bayonne & Saint-Jean-Pied-de-Port to Santiago de Compostela

1,160 kilometres

Detailed in Chapters 1 to 14

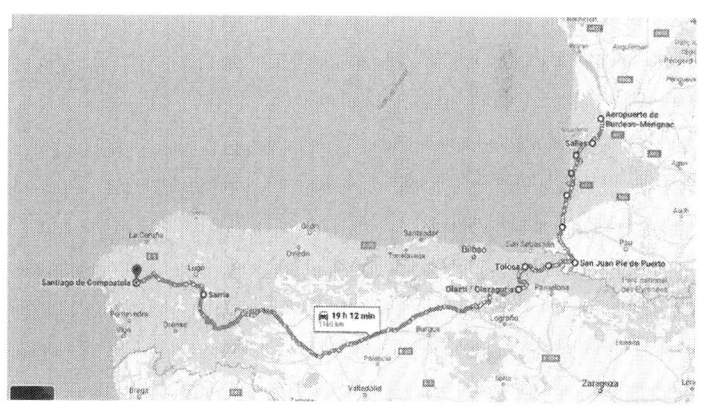

Credit Google Maps

Route 3

Saint-Jean-Pied-de-Port to Santiago de Compostela

850 kilometres

Detailed in chapters 5 to 14

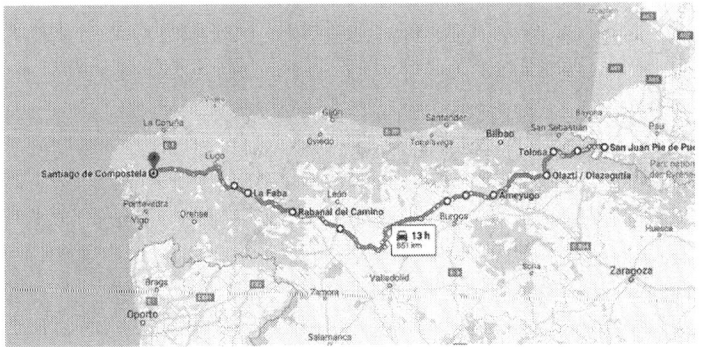

Credit Google Maps

Route 4

Carrion de los Condes to Santiago de Compostela

425 kilometres

Detailed in chapters 10 to 14

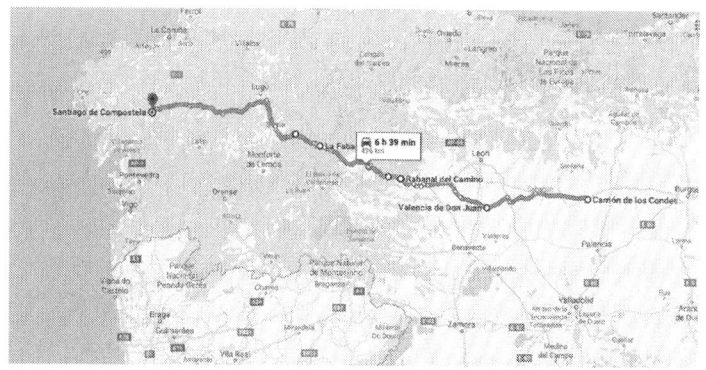

Credit Google Maps

Route 5

Astorga to Santiago de Compostela

285 kilometres

Detailed in chapters 11 to 14

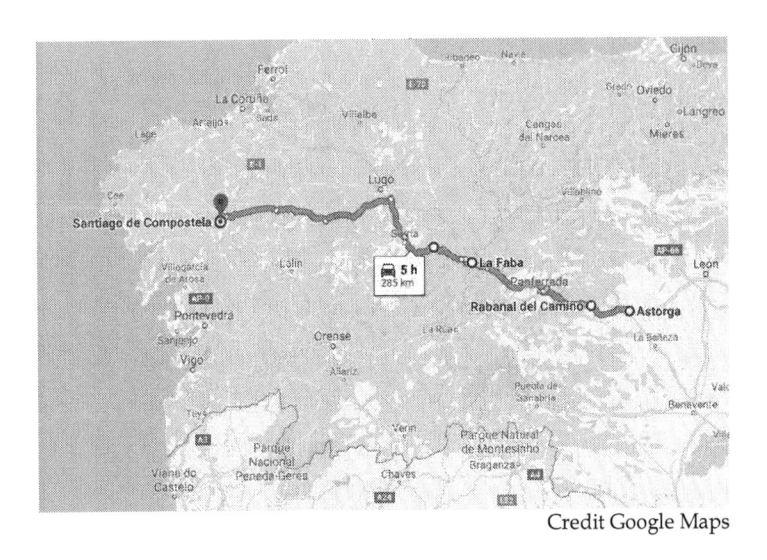

Credit Google Maps

Preparation

Ideally, your preparation for the Camino should begin 12 months before your intended travel date. Don't forget, there is a lot more planning involved in taking a bike on the Camino than when you walk it. You can cover so much more ground than a hiker and our route, which we covered in two weeks, would have taken the average hiker at least six weeks. But the downside is that you are more prone to experience the odd accident and you have to be a lot fitter and tougher than the average walker.

We met quite elderly walkers on the Camino, people who were overweight and some who were positively obese. A lot of walkers were challenging themselves to get fit, which is great, but it's fair to say that being significantly overweight or unfit is simply not an option for the cyclist who wants to cover some decent distance.

There were a lot more climbs than I had initially anticipated, and quitting is not an option if you want to make it to the next planned stopover where a bed for the night and a plate of hot food beckons.

It is therefore essential to set out a decent training regime, one that prepares you for the eventualities of cycling your chosen kilometre target with gradients on some days that would test a professional on the Tour de France.

First, you need to work out what your average

daily distance is going to be and for how long you are going to cycle. I've already said that our group was middle-aged and on reflection, I think we were over-ambitious in deciding to complete 1,000 km in 14 days. Although we did manage to meet our target, some days we were pushed to our physical and mental limits. Two days, in particular, a couple of members of the group could have ended up in serious trouble. I daresay there are young cyclists in their twenties and thirties who want to do more than the 1,000 km or more than 100 km a day. Likewise, there are cyclists who perhaps just want to spend a few more hours in the café at lunchtime, or perhaps are ready to call it a day by early afternoon and in my opinion that's just great.

The beauty of a bike is that you can cover more ground. That was my primary reason for choosing to bike the route rather than to walk it. The reality was that I didn't have six weeks or eight weeks to spare. Good luck to those who have, but for me, two weeks on a bike with the wind in my face, building up my fitness levels and losing weight along The Way, was the perfect way to complete 1,000 kilometres of the Camino.

So, back to your daily mileage. I assume because you have bought this book that you cycle on a fairly regular basis. Now, this is important in choosing how many miles or kilometres you wish to average daily. I want you to think about some of your recent runs. I want you to try and recall some of your favourite routes, think about the distance and the gradient but more importantly I want you to remember some of those days where perhaps you overdid it and wondered what the hell you were doing on a bike when you could be tucked up in a pub enjoying a nice beer with your mates. We have all had those days.

For example, there is a route close to my home in Altea, Spain, that is 107 km with an ascent of nearly 2,300 m. I do this route on my race bike three or four times a year, and I certainly do not do anything longer, because I'm just about running on reserve by the time I get home.

Now, while I love every minute (almost) of that ride and I have an enormous sense of achievement at the end, I know that it pushes me to my physical limit. It therefore stands to reason that while you can cycle these kinds of distances with that kind of elevation for one day, you wouldn't want to do it for two or three weeks, especially not with 25 kilos of bike and kit underneath you.

That is THE biggest mistake Camino cyclists make.

I nearly fell into that trap too. I knew I could cycle 100 km in a day so I added a few into our route, completely forgetting about the weight we were carrying or the fact we had cycled five or six days in a row. Some days we were still cycling and looking for accommodation at seven or eight o'clock in the evening and the enjoyment of the day had been sucked right out of us. On those days, you wonder what the hell you are doing.

The golden rule is to enjoy your cycling, take it easy, take in the sights and sounds around you and don't bust your gut trying to push in ridiculous amounts of kilometres. If you come across a nice café with a tasty menu del día, sit down and enjoy it and don't feel guilty about taking an extra hour there while you wait for your food to digest.

What is a sensible level of daily kilometres, readers often ask on our Facebook group **(Camino de Santiago Cycle Challenge)**. Well, that's where your preparation and training come in because the golden rule is always to listen to your body. Remember, at the beginning of this chapter, I asked you to try and remember some of your favourite rides.

You might love that run from your hometown in Keswick, Cumbria, over to Penrith, Low Hesket and back in a circular route around Bassenthwaite Lake and back down into Keswick. It's a 62-mile circular route with 3,000 feet elevation taking in some of the most beautiful scenery in England.

Now, this is the crucial part: can you envisage doing that ride for seven days in a row and not on your favourite race bike but a heavier mountain bike or hybrid, loaded up with at least 10 kg of kit? Here is the key question: after you get home from that ride do you believe hand on heart that you could push in another 20 km if you had to?

One of my favourite runs from the beach where I live takes me on a rather flat route towards Benidorm before making a sharp right and heading for the hills of Finestrat. By the time I reach Finestrat and head towards Relleu, I hit the mountains and it can be a long hot day. From Relleu I take the road to Aigues, (more climbing) and eventually head downhill for a gentle 20 km back to base. It's an 82 km ride with a 900 m elevation. Nice, but bloody tough, especially on a hot day. And could I then go out and do another 20 km? Probably, but only just.

Listen to your body. There is no 'ideal' average mileage and it depends on the individual. However, the formula is to think of your favourite ride and base your average distance on that. Whatever you do, DON'T take your longest training run and think that you can achieve that sort of mileage every day. You may well do it, but you won't enjoy the experience, I guarantee it.

I planned to average around 80 km a day and on reflection 65-70 km would have been more sensible and given us a lot more time to enjoy the scenery and nights out at various hostelries and *albergues*. On a couple of occasions, we barely had the energy to lift a beer glass to our lips. Don't make the same mistake. That's why you have bought this book. Listen to your body and listen to Scotty.

On a positive note, you don't have to be a seasoned cyclist to enjoy or take part in a cycle challenge on the Camino. One of our group, Caroline, hadn't been on a bike for 35 years, but she was determined to take part in the challenge and raise money for Marie Curie Cancer Care as she had lost her father to cancer in 2018.

We had 12 months to train her, but she didn't even have a bike. The following day we travelled to our local Decathlon store and purchased a bike for her and it was game on, time to start the training.

I introduced a gentle, sensible and paced training regime to Caroline as I didn't want to put her off. It was somewhat different from my first few training runs after I had given up football at the age of 51. I was getting weary and 90-minute games of football were taking their toll on my old body, especially after I had been getting lumps kicked out of me from the age of ten. I'd wake up the day after a game and ease myself out of bed. My knees ached, my ankles ached and because of a stiff back, I could hardly make it to the shower.

"Give it up," my wife would advise.

"She's right," my daughter echoed in the background.

I knew it made sense as it was getting harder and harder and yet it was my only real exercise of the week. I envisaged morphing into a couch potato, piling on the pounds while I drank far too much beer.

My rescue came in the form of my cousin, Neil Bryson who was travelling to the Costa Blanca with his cycling club.

"I'll bring you a bike," he said, "give cycling a try, you old bastard."

"It's a deal," I replied.

And so I travelled out daily with the group from

the Lake District in England, average age 65. By the end of the week they had planned their 'big day,' the 107 km ballbuster.

"I'm in the gang," I shouted, "not a chance," came the reply from the group leader, "you need months of training leading up to a climb like that." But one thing I am not short of is determination and sheer stubbornness and despite his protestations, I was indeed *in the gang*.

He wasn't going to stop me; he didn't own the roads.

I'll admit that he was probably right. The ride nearly killed me and even though it was early April, the temperature that day was brutal. There were three bitches of climbs, all of which were around 600 m. The last one up to a place called Confrides after 60 km in the saddle was never-ending torture, but nevertheless I took my time, lots of rests and made it because I knew the terrain and I knew that if I made 10 km of painful ascent, the remaining 27 km were more or less all downhill.

It was tough, but I was proud of myself that day. I had proved to the group leader that I could do it and despite a few aches and pains and a little sunstroke, I felt like a million dollars. However, the most amazing thing happened to me the next morning. I got out of bed and I still felt like a million dollars. A few of my leg muscles hurt, but there was no pain in any of my joints and as I walked around the house that morning I felt like I was floating on air.

That was it, I was hooked. I had found a new sport and the following week I went out and purchased a second hand Bergamont race bike. The rest, they say is history, but Caroline would get a far gentler introduction to cycling.

Twelve Month Training Schedule

It was nearly four months before I introduced Caroline to a ride like the 107 km ballbuster. We took it easy at first as I didn't want to frighten her, so we started with a couple of flatties, 25 km to Benidorm and back. I gradually introduced her to hills, always bearing in mind she was on a bike twice the weight of mine and with mountain bike tyres. We made a point of trying to get out twice a week and steadily increased the mileage. We went off-road too, along the River Algar near where we live. Others joined us on our training rides because they had heard of our challenge and wanted to be part of it. As word spread, I had interested parties joining our Facebook group, contemplating the challenge. They came in from the UK, Spain, Norway, South Africa and even one from Australia.

Three months in we were regularly cycling 50 km plus on each run.

As the months ticked by, most people skipped their training sessions or quit before they had hardly started. But Caroline stuck with it and announced she wanted to raise money for charity. Another of my old mates from Newcastle was also making serious noises about joining the challenge. When push came to shove, we had a total of just four cyclists ready and willing and committed to a fortnight at the end of June. We talked about and plotted our route, and as the date drew nearer, we started to get excited and got the maps out and checked the type of accommodation along the way.

We chose Bordeaux as the starting point because it has an airport and seemed like the logical place to get the 1,000 kilometres in, and it was wine country so Caroline needed no further persuasion. I checked with the boys, who would have to get two flights from England, but it was doable and not too expensive. Caroline and I booked a Ryanair flight from Valencia at the extortionate price of 17€. What a result!

We upped our training schedule, bought bike racks and panniers and filled them up in an attempt to get used to the weight. It's a hell of a difference cycling on an unladen race bike to travelling around on a heavier bike with luggage.

With just a few months to go Caroline and I were cycling 60 km through the mountains, twice a week, loaded up. The boys back home in Newcastle were doing the same. It was time to up the ante and we planned a week's training camp six weeks before the trip. Dave flew in from Newcastle and hired a bike from our local cycle hire shop, Top Bikes.

Cycling two or three times a week is all very well, but research told us that in order to complete the challenge we had to train back to back and had to cycle at least four days in a row, averaging the sort of mileage we planned to do on the Camino, otherwise, we were wasting our time.

Only by doing that do you appreciate just how hard it is cycling day after day. Some people's bodies are unfortunately just not up for that sort of physical endurance.

We started easy on the six-day camp, two long flatties without kit and then headed to the mountains with our bikes fully laden. We managed six consecutive days including the 107 km ballbuster and even though that day nearly broke poor Caroline, she rang the following day and said she was feeling fine and couldn't wait to begin our challenge.

I reassured her that there wouldn't be any days on the Camino that would be anywhere near as hard as the shift she had just put in the previous day. How I wish I had never allowed those words to tumble out of my mouth. She would ultimately throw them in my face on more than one occasion.

Your Bike and Luggage

At the risk of repeating myself too much, it's all about travelling light and choosing the right type of bike. If you intend to do a serious amount of mileage and sleep en route, you want to choose a sturdy touring bike. Even if you intend to 'tarmac' the route the whole way, there are times you will have no option but to jump onto a rough cycle track. A decent mountain bike with slicks or hybrid tyres is a must. Forget your race bike unless you have a backup support vehicle following on behind carrying your essential kit.

Step forward the 'Rock Rider 520.'

I cannot speak highly enough of this bike. It has the perfect riding position, double disc brakes and suspension and with a little cleaning and maintenance a couple of times a week, it never faltered once. I didn't even need to adjust the gears during the whole trip.

A back rack with decent size panniers and a decent handlebar front bag was more than enough to pack my kit into without the need for front wheel panniers too. I've cycled with those bad boys on my front forks before, it's too much weight and very cumbersome though I do accept if you intend to camp and cook each evening, they are probably necessary. Not for our intrepid group though, it was bars and restaurants each night for us!

I also cycled with a small cross bar bag containing my phone, chargers, toiletries, energy gels and snacks.

Essential Kit

I think any serious cyclist will know what they should be taking on a long-distance expedition. However, it's a good idea to discuss this list with your fellow travellers and push it on your Facebook Group.

Sleeping Bag and Tent or Bivvy Bag
Two pair of cycle shorts
Two Cycling tops
Two Pair cycling socks.
Cycle shoes
Evening wear
Towel and toiletries
Spare water bottle
First aid kit
Moisturiser
Flip flops
Light trainers
Dry Bags
Waterproofs
Plastic ties
Tools
Spare tubes
Spare chain links
Swiss Army Knife
Torch
Needle and Thread

TRANSPORT

Getting there and back

Whatever mode of transport you consider keep in mind that, if you take your bike with you, you have to get it back home again. You have two options at Santiago. You can take the bike with you on your chosen mode of transport or leave the hassle to someone else by simply handing it in to and office or depot. They will deliver your bike within a few days, right to your door. The good news is that there are plenty of companies in Santiago who will do just that.

By Air

If you are flying your bike home, you will need to check with the Airline or Airlines you are flying with. If you do not have a direct flight home make sure you check out the conditions on ALL of your flights. The costs and weight restrictions all vary. You need to box your bike and you can buy a box in Santiago and do it yourself or pay to have it boxed at the airport. You can cycle to the airport but if you are taking a taxi, make sure you book one with a large boot. Check first.

If you have a direct flight to your home airport, then taking your bike on board the aircraft will be the cheapest and easiest option for you, generally between 50 and 70€. If you have to use more than one airline to get home, then I suggest you look at an independent transporter.

Santiago airport operates flights to all of the major connecting international airports such as Madrid, Barcelona, Lisbon and London. Other direct destinations include Alicante, Amsterdam, Alghero, Bilbao, Basel, Brussels, Dublin, Frankfurt, Fuerteventura, Geneva, Gran Canarias, Lanzarote, Madeira, Malaga, Menorca, Milan, Palma Majorca, Paris, Rome, Seville, Tenerife, Valencia and Zurich.

Train

The Spanish train network is among the best in the world and most trains operate a 'wheel your bike on' policy. But if you want to travel by high-speed train (AVE) there are restrictions, i.e. you have to box up your bike.

There are high-speed rail links to major airports in the north of Spain, to Madrid and Bilbao who operate International flights and to Porto in Portugal. There are also high-speed trains that will take you to the ferry ports of Bilbao and Santander who operate ferries to the UK, Ireland and France.

The Bus

You can take a Spanish bus anywhere in Europe and they are cheap, reliable and luxurious. They have air-con and a video screen in the back of all seats and most of them have free Wi-Fi. If, for example, you wanted to book your bus to London from the bus station in Santiago then they will plan the cheapest and quickest option possible. It's not everyone's idea of the best way to get home, but they are bicycle-friendly, and you can get your bike on the bus for next to nothing. You do have to have your bike in a carry case or wrapped. They sell lightweight bike sacks for 12€ at all bus stations.

Independent Transport Companies

You can send your bike home from Santiago and there are plenty companies who will do this for you. Costs vary depending on your final destination.

SEUR is a Spanish courier company and it ships bikes internationally. It has offices in Santiago and you will simply need to wheel your bike into the office and the company does the rest. They charge 46€ to ship your bike anywhere in Spain, but international prices vary depending on your final destination. For example, Jan Vandersypen sent his electric bike (heavier) back home to Belgium for 92€.

UPS also have offices in the city and a post office in the old part of town, near the cathedral, can also send your bike home. A bike to London will cost around 80€ including panniers and helmet.

You may also wish to contact Velocipedo, they

have good reviews on all of the Camino Cycle Forums.

Their website is ww.welvelocipedo.com.

And finally...

I do hope you have enjoyed the read, the information, the top tips and the explanations and details of the routes. I'd welcome any comments about the book on my website, **www.kenscottbooks.com** or you can email me at **kenscottbooks@gmail.com**. You will also find details of my other books on the site.

I won't dwell on the disappointment of the group splitting up in Santiago. As Jan said, everyone has their own idea of what the Camino means and if an individual makes it to Santiago, sees the cathedral and then decides he wants to hotfoot it back home, then so be it.

The bus journey back to Alicante was a good one for me. I relaxed, dozed a little and managed to read two books on my Kindle. While the Camino was a great adventure, when cycling it you always have to be on the ball, you have to plan ahead and concentrate every turn of your wheel. As I sank back into the plush leather seat of the bus, it was as if someone had turned on a maximum relax switch and I was almost looking forward to the 14 or so hours travelling back. Fourteen hours where I could do as I pleased for once in a fortnight.

Getting off the bus wasn't such a joy though. I had seized up and I was stiff as a board; the old joints not as flexible as they used to be.

But within a couple of days, I was back to normal and I have to say I was feeling great. Despite eating and drinking whatever I wanted during the trip, I had lost 5 kg. What a result and two days later I put my bike together and took off on a short training run.

There is no way to describe how great it felt cycling without any kit attached to my bike, and with leg muscles far stronger as a result of 14 days in the saddle I felt like I was ready for the Tour de France.

There was no doubt about it, the Camino Challenge had transported me back to a fitness level I last enjoyed ten years ago.

And now that it's over, what does the Camino de Santiago mean to me and more importantly, am I planning a quick return visit?

I can understand the attraction of returning to the Camino each year; it's such a special experience and something that you can't relate to until you have been there and the answer is yes, I want to go back there soon.

I also have a desire to walk some of the Camino some day. As much as I love cycling, I like hiking too and one day hope to experience it on two legs instead of two wheels. We met a few families en route and that appeals to me too, my daughter said she would love to spend a week or two on the Camino as it's not too far from her home in Salamanca.

As I've said all along, we were not pro cyclists and we certainly didn't do this challenge correctly. But we did it and if we can do it, with the right preparation and training there's no reason why anyone can't enjoy at least a few hundred kilometres cycling the Camino.

We used all types of accommodation from campsites to hotels and everything in between and we planned everything ourselves. For a price, there are companies who will do it all for you and provide guides and back up vehicles too. Let's be honest, we all want a hassle-free way to cycle 'The Way.'

All four of us researched the hell out of the internet prior to our trip and we couldn't find anything that suited us at a reasonable price. One company who offered a 350 km guided tour wanted 2,850€ per person for a five-day trip! Granted, they were staying in nice hotels each night but we all agreed that to really be a part of the spiritual journey there has to be an element of hardship and discomfort, otherwise what's the point?

We arrived at the conclusion that the ideal experience would involve a couple of nights camping but a few nights of luxury too. And we wanted to cut out the hassle of transporting our bikes over thousands of kilometres. We wanted nice food, drinks and a good crowd to cycle with. Above all we agreed that we wanted a challenge but we wanted fun and a good old laugh.

There were plenty of cycle companies offering 4- and 5-day trips, 50 km per day but that wasn't for us. We wondered; would it be possible to pull together the 'perfect' Camino Cycle challenge at a reasonable price? Well, we decided to give it a try and we think we may have cracked it.

The Camino de Santiago Cycle Challenge

I am happy to announce that since we have returned from our Camino Challenge, we have formed a company with a team of like-minded individuals to offer you, the cyclist, the chance to share in our experiences on the Camino de Santiago.

We don't want to cycle with Chris Froome or Egan Bernal and although we certainly wouldn't want to discourage any fit twenty-year olds from joining us, our Camino Cycling Packages are aimed at the middle aged, reasonably fit cyclist, 35 – 40 plus, who perhaps gets out just once or twice a week on a run. We also want to encourage the type of person like Caroline, who had never been on a bike for donkey's years but was up for the challenge. With the right preparation and training why not?

Make no mistake, these challenges won't be park rides.

I detail below one of our 450 km challenges over seven days. As you can see, we will be averaging 65 km per day with an average elevation per day of 600 m.

For further details of the tour, join and check out our Facebook Group, **Camino de Santiago Cycle Challenge** and drop us your email if you are interested. We will send you our newsletter too.

www.caminocyclechallenge.com
caminocyclechallenge@gmail.com

We've looked at the routes and the terrain and of course the accommodation and we will be mixing that up with a little camping, country hotels and perhaps one night in an albergue. Staying in an albergue isn't everyone's idea of fun but for the craic, we suggest it must be experienced if for no other reason than to talk about it over dinner one evening.

We all agreed that carrying so much kit was a pain in the ass. So even though we plan a couple of days at campsites, your tents and sleeping bags (and your other kit) will be carried by our support vehicle. We will provide all of your camping kit. You won't have to worry about transportation of your bike either as we will supply the bikes. We will have a mobile mechanic as a back-up AND spare bikes if your bike decides to call it a day.

Looking back and taking stock and analysing each day of the experience, those early few days, when we knew where we were staying each night, knowing that we had a bed for the night and a guarantee of hot food (and some beer and wine) were without a doubt the most relaxing. Even on a long, tough cycling day, if we knew there was a guaranteed pleasant end to the day, we'd push ourselves to get there.

All of the places we will be staying at will have been checked out by our team, the campsites will be fully equipped with decent showers and washing facilities and bars and restaurants within walking distance, if not on site. The dates of the Camino Challenge and more information will be published in our newsletter and on our website and Facebook page.

We hope to bring the package in at around 1,350€ per person and group discounts are available.
Our itinerary will look something like this:

Saturday. Meet at Campsite El Eden, Carrion de los Condes. Your tents will be assembled. We supply one and two-person tents. Larger tents for groups are available by prior arrangement.
Welcome reception and dinner at 20.00 pm.

Sunday. Cycle 65 km. Elevation 200 m. Evening in hotel or private Airbnb residence in of Mayorga.

Monday. Cycle. 65 km. Elevation 250 m. Evening in hotel or private Airbnb residence in Hospital de Órbigo.

Tuesday. Cycle. 56 km. Elevation 560 m. Evening in hotel or private Airbnb residence in Bembibre.

Wednesday. 60 km. Elevation 430 m. Evening in albergue in Vega de Valcarce.

Thursday. 52 km. Elevation 1,100 m. Evening in hotel or private Airbnb residence in Sarria.

Friday. Cycle 62 km. Elevation 1,050 m. Evening in hotel or private Airbnb residence in Melide.

Saturday. 60 km. Elevation 685 m. Evening camping in location of Santiago de Compostela. Farewell dinner.

Sunday. Breakfast and Adios

Please note, accommodation is subject to change and flights are not included. Airports within easy reach of Carrion de los Condes are Bilbao, Burgos, Valladolid and Madrid. Spanish trains and the Alsa buses offer a regular service direct to Carrion de los Condes or Palencia which is thirty minutes by taxi .
For the return journey, Santiago de Compostela is an international airport, Madrid and Porto airports are easily accessible by train and bus.
I do hope you will consider joining us.

It was rewarding getting to Santiago without support of any kind and if you do decide to do it independently, good luck to you. I hope you make it safely to your end destination and you have fun along the way. Likewise, if you decide to join us on one of our group challenges, I promise that we will eliminate some of the errors that you have read about in this book. Hindsight is a wonderful thing of course but it's a fact, every day cycling along The Way, you learn something new. The adventure also teaches you a little more about yourself as a person, what you are capable of and how you cope with some of crap that such an undertaking can throw your way.

I believe that now we have experienced life on two wheels on the Camino, next time we can eliminate most of the 'downs,' and yet at the same time not take away any of the excitement.

As for next year's challenge, if you would like to join us, you can sign up on our Facebook group, **Camino de Santiago Cycle Challenge**, and with what we have learned during this year's Camino, I guarantee it will run a lot smoother. Send us an email to sign up for the newsletter.

There will also be a video to accompany this book; it will be posted on the Facebook Group and YouTube in due course. You can find all of the photographs from our challenge on our Facebook group. It will give you a nice taste of what we went through.

And finally, if you have enjoyed the read and found this book useful, please don't forget to leave a review on Amazon. Who knows, perhaps we'll be seeing you soon. Happy cycling.

Epilogue

And yes, Diane and Chris Jackson were as good as their word. They travelled the miles and made it down to a campsite in Benidorm. On the day of our welcome home party at ´The Church Bar´ in Albir we had a wonderful surprise when they walked into the bar smiling broadly. We had known them no longer than twelve hours and yet they came good. We were as glad to see them as they were to see us and despite the throngs of people who had come along to welcome us (and sponsor us) we found a table and sat with them for most of the day. It was a perfect end to our journey along the Camino.

Fortis
Publishing Services

DID YOU LIKE THIS BOOK?

Visit our online store for more books like this one.

www.fortispublishing.co.uk

Printed in Great Britain
by Amazon